First paperback edition August 2019

First electronic edition August 2019

Written by Tim Bean and staff

Layout and cover design by Tim Bean, 2019

Published by Nicholas T. Orange

www.orangebeanindiana.com

From the pages of orangebeanindiana.com

Inventing Indiana

The events and individuals that shaped
Hoosier culture, one story at a time...

Stories by Tim Bean and staff
Published by Nicholas T. Orange

For our Readers.
Thanks for two great years
And here's to twenty more

Nick & Tim

Table of Contents

Who is OrangeBean? 1

Damage, Delay, and Destruction: Indiana's 2018 Flood 2

Popcorn: a Medley of Facts, Physics and Flavors 5

Humans & Floodplains: A Love/Hate Story 8

Indiana's Claim to Lincoln 11

Indiana: First and Last 14

in Rotary Jails 14

The First Theme Park: Santa Claus Land 17

Indiana, the Birthplace 20

of Professional Baseball 20

Slabs of Stone 23

Indy's Museum of Psychphonics 26

'A Christmas Story': Nostalgia, Ad Nauseam 28

The Midwest's First 33

Long-Distance Auto Race 33

Three Girls Gone: the Ford Pinto and Indiana v. Ford Motor Co. 37

Mediums in the Midwest: the American Spiritualism Movement 47

Before the Detroit Pistons, We Had the Fort Wayne-Zollner Pistons 51

Business Outside, Opulent Inside: the Evansville Victory Theatre 54

Indiana's Mysterious and Marvelous Toy Fairy 58

The 1910 Kingsland Wreck: Indiana's Worst 60

Interurban Train Disaster 60

What is the Kokomo Hum? 63

Bigfoot in Indiana? 70

The Indiana City that 77

Once Defined America

77

Browse Vincennes' Rare Book Collection

81

Hoosier Cabinets: The Swiss Army Knife of American Cabinetry

84

From Field to Food: Three Historic Grist Mills

88

"If It Flies, It Dies": Exploring Indiana's C-47 Nike Missile Site

92

Nike Missile Bases in the Movies

104

The South Bend Mansion Built by a Plow

112

Indiana Invention:

116

Stove Top Stuffing

116

Unsolved: Indy's 1978 Burger Chef Murders

120

Oops: Hexavalent Chromium Taints Lake Michigan

124

Gary Own's Lee Calhoun

127

Songwriter Cole Porter: from Indiana to Broadway

132

E.W. Kelley: Indiana's Food Industry Emperor

136

Injury This Bird, Go Directly to Jail

140

Gimbel's Taught America How to Shop

145

The Most Dangerous Animal in North America? Bambi.

149

Indiana, Welcome to Tornado Alley

155

The Indiana Bridge Stolen a Pound at a Time

158

UFO over Southern Indiana?

163

Seymour Mastodon Finds Home at Indiana State Museum

167

The Complex History of the Governor's Mansion(s)

171

The Problem with Potholes

176

Indiana's Historic Roberts Settlement

185

When Indianapolis Saved the Life of a President

189

The Short Life of the White City Amusement Park

195

President W. H. Harrison's Historic Grouseland   200

Delicious, Delectable, and Disgusting Indiana Dishes   204

Indiana's Open-Air School Experiment   212

One Hoosier, Thousands of Lives   215

Kokomo, Indiana: The "City of Firsts"   219

Evansville's Legendary Bosse Field   223

Made in America, Made in Indiana   227

Zombie-Style History: Exploring Abandoned Indiana   234

The Sweet, Stinky, and Sticky Life of Maple Syrup   243

Lassen Pavilion and Indiana's Early "Party Town"   248

Thornless Roses and the Krider World's Fair Garden of Middlebury   252

The Unsolved Murder of Dr. Helen Knabe   256

Indiana-made Gatorade: The Go-To Drink of NFL & Elvis   261

Indiana Insects to Avoid: the Pesky, Painful, and Possibly Fatal   264

Who is OrangeBean?

OrangeBean started in a Northwest Indiana Starbucks as a whimsical idea for a news aggregate. Half a decade later, there's now a whimsical website, a whimsical LLC, a whimsical Facebook page, and now a whimsical collection of stories.

Nicholas Orange is an entrepreneur, business owner, therapist and minister currently living in Indianapolis. Among his business ventures is co-ownership of Family and Community Partners and Family and Community Solutions, counseling agencies serving central Indiana. Nick is also blessed to be an Associate Pastor and Minister of Pastoral Care at First Christian Church of Beech Grove. He received his BA in Political Science from Purdue Northwest, and then an MDiv and MA from Christian Theological Seminary in Indianapolis. He is currently working on his MBA.

Tim Bean has a BA from Purdue Northwest somewhere around the house along with a few writing awards. He is lucky to have two headstrong children he adores, a lovely wife he doesn't deserve, many woodworking tools, a custom drum kit, and his trusty MacBook.

Damage, Delay, and Destruction: Indiana's 2018 Flood

DOWNED TREES CLOGGING DEEP RIVER

By Tim Bean

For most Hoosiers in northern Indiana, the flood damage in 2018 manifested as flooded basements and difficult commutes. Some Hoosiers were hit harder than others, and some (yours truly) had to deal with the flood both at home and at work. Mother Nature's version of an alley-oop.

At work, I witnessed the awesome results of a Millenia flood (I officially call it that) on the serpentine shores of Deep River in Northwest Indiana. The centerpiece of the 1300-acre Deep

2

River County Park, Deep River itself is a shallow, slow-moving river that attracts thousands of sightseers, hikers and canoes every year, typically in the spring and summer.

Sightseers and hikers didn't feel the sting of the 2018 flood, but anyone manning a canoe or kayak sure did. Trees didn't fall into Deep River; they marched into it like lemmings. Hundreds of trees now straddle and choke the river, from tumbleweed masses of scrub trees to ancient maples with initials carved into the sapwood. The heavy machinery needed to clear these blockages can't traverse the dense woods around the river, so time and erosion are the only tools park staff has.

Park workers and a handful of volunteers are clearing the flood's flotsam from the Deep River visitors' areas and park trails. The cat's cradle of lumber dominating the twists and turns of Deep River haven't even been touched yet, because the routine park maintenance must go on.

There's no need to worry about the river itself. Rivers have ways of keeping themselves clean, even from the notorious pollution of the northern Calumet. Flood waters are fast and fast waters are healthy. The blockages won't last long against the fast river, flowing up, over, around and through any object. Water made the Grand Canyon. It can handle a birch tree.

That doesn't hold true for the river's native fish. Fishing in the river this year will be interesting. Will the fish get choked and suffocate or starve in muddy pockets and eddies, or will enthusiasts find hundreds of new sweet spots to cast into? It could go either way.

The flood certainly abridged the popular canoe trips down the picturesque river. From the launch area in the county park, boaters can enjoy five to ten minutes of moving water—then they'll hit the first impassable mass, resembling a beaver dam on steroids.

Removing the massive jams involves several workers, chainsaws, excavators, waders, and lots of cussing. No one wants to hop in a flowing river with a fifty-pound chainsaw and wrestle it through a two-foot thick oak while maintaining their balance against the river's tug.

The flood didn't just unearth logs and sticks. Sandy deposits buried the grassy paths and landscaping of the park proper, exposing or destroying delicate root systems of the landscaping. Now devoid of dirt, these landscaping dry sockets must be refilled with fresh soil then replanted. It's arduous work. Park employees slog home tired and sore, hands red with blisters from shoveling, raking, lifting and dragging.

No one is complaining, mind you. Those that work at the park or volunteer do it for a reason. We love county parks. But, damn, I hope it doesn't flood again for awhile. I don't think our backs can take it.

*I would like to add that two weeks after writing this article, I had a back spasm and missed two days of work. I dedicate (and attribute) that spasm to flood cleanup, and would like to wish it an unprintable string of curse words.

Popcorn: a Medley of Facts, Physics and Flavors

By Tim Bean

Despite being a lifelong Hoosier, I never "got into" popcorn. I rarely ate it at home and never bought it at movie theaters (the theater's "butter" topping looked like something I'd put in a car transmission).

My preferences aside, I've realized thousands of jobs and billions of dollars are connected to the popcorn industry in Indiana alone. As a proud Hoosier, I chased the topic a little more and dug up some interesting "kernels" of trivia about America's favorite snack food.

Here's some industrial popcorn terminology: A *kernel* is an unpopped popcorn. A *flake* is a popped kernel. Popcorn refers to multiple kernels or flakes. Kernels that fail to pop are called *old maids* and kernels that partially pop are *bridesmaids*. Most commercially-sold popcorn is of the yellow or white varieties.

Forget precious metals and buy some Jiffypop.

The average retail markup for movie theater popcorn is over 1300%, making a fifty-cent investment worth $6. Nothing has that kind of profit margin. Not even gold.

Popcorn isn't created equal.

The shape of popcorn often determines its purpose. Butterfly-shaped popcorn is preferred for freshly-consumed snacks, such as microwave or movie theater varieties, while the hardier, mushroom-shaped type finds homes in caramel corn or bagged snacks.

I'll stick with my Lucky Charms.

In the 1800s, popcorn, cream and sugar became a staple breakfast food. Gradually, boxed cereals replaced popcorn in American homes, but popcorn's influence in the breakfast market still echoes today (Corn Pops?).

Clogs your heart quicker than superglue.

Popcorn alone is an excellent healthy snack, but those chowing down on a buttered bag should realize those toppings add almost 30 grams of saturated fat. You'd be healthier topping your popcorn with a Snickers bar.

The physics of popcorn.

Unpopped kernels are caused from slight imperfections in the tough hull or uneven heating, which prevent the kernel's interior from achieving the high pressure needed to pop.

Packing with popcorn.

Several shipping companies are researching popcorn as a plentiful, biodegradable packing material, but its susceptibility to moisture and pests have made it difficult. Research continues, and popcorn may provide a solution to the packing problem.

Don't try this at home.

In 1941, botanist Thomas Goodspeed once heated thousand-year-old kernels from a Chilean archeological dig site. They popped up perfectly, although tasted pretty bland.

Thanks, Mesoamerica!

Before selective breeding around six thousand years ago, corn was originally a grass with cobs smaller than your pinky, and sported about ten tasteless kernels. Fast forward to today, and the average cob is ten times larger, with eight hundred sugary-sweet kernels.

Humans & Floodplains: A Love/Hate Story

By Tim Bean

Humans love floodplains. We always have and we always will.

We love them for the abundance of freshwater they provide since humans coalesced into towns, then cities. We love them for the rich deposits of nutrients left behind by receding waters. We love them for the nearby waterways for transportation and trade, and we love the miles and miles of flatlands of the floodplains, which is both easy to traverse and build on.

We love floodplains, but we HATE flooding.

Everyone in Indiana has a flood story or two to share, and efforts to top one another in these watery tales always crests after a recent flood. Before we tell our fish stories of flooding (I once caught one THIS big), we should stop to consider why we stumble through these flooding emergencies.

To start with, it's our fault. That's not a popular thing to say, but it's true, especially in northern Indiana. Almost the entirety of northern Indiana is a giant floodplain, scrapped flat by the Lake Chicago glacier thousands of years ago.

That flatland eventually became marshlands straddling a variety of waterways, but after settlers hacked out the first homes in the wilderness over two centuries ago, that marshland became farmland (Manifest Destiny and all that). Human ingenuity can alter the purpose of our surrounding landscape, but rarely changes the landscape itself. This means flooding.

Marshlands that once soaked up the overflow of rivers has become flat grasslands or pavement. Neither absorbs water well. River overflow that once spread out only a few yards now spreads out hundreds of yards. Sewer and storm drain systems are no match either, even with millions of dollars in infrastructure engineering. Even the best sewer can't match the efficiency of nature's spongy marshes and wetlands.

All this flooding seen in 2018 and 2019, from flooded basements to floating roads, is a direct result of human shortsightedness and residential construction. That's not supposition or speculation. That is a fact, Jack. All of Indiana's efforts to build cities, towns, and roads bracketed our waterways with these artificial flatlands, and the water just spreads like the Nile delta.

Describing the these deluges in extraordinary terms (a Hundred-Year Flood or a Ten-Year Flood) reframes human culpability as "bad luck." Lately, I've heard the 2018 flood called a "Five-Hundred-Year Flood." Folks, they are just making that stuff up.

Rising population density, rising construction, destruction of natural areas, and an increase in precipitation are at fault, all of which rest squarely on the feet of humans. Flooding will become more destructive and frequent. Soon, we'll be having a Five-Hundred Year Flood every two or three years. Or even every year. Imagine that.

Indiana's Claim to Lincoln

By Tim Bean

Three states (and one nation) can proudly tout themselves "Lincoln's Home": Kentucky, the Birthplace of Lincoln; Indiana, the Boyhood Home of Lincoln; and Illinois, the Land of Lincoln. Considered by the public and historians to be the greatest president in history, groups readily hope to identify with the 16th president. For example, today's Republican Party frequently refers to itself as the "Party of Lincoln," although the GOP of 1860 would be unrecognizable today. There's also the Lincoln Motor Company, an aircraft carrier, a submarine. More recently, there's been a vampire hunter.

In this mess of namesakes, what's Indiana's part?

Lincoln family moved from Knob Creek, Kentucky, to what would be Spencer County, Indiana, in 1816, the year Indiana gained statehood. Lincoln's father laid claim to 80 acres and, with his son's help, cleared the land of trees and used the wood for a log cabin. The land was reasonably fertile and a nearby water source made it hospitable.

Two years after arriving, Nancy Lincoln, died of milk sickness (a rare illness even in the 1800s). Ten years later, his sister Sarah would die in child birth. Death on the frontier was commonplace, but the loss of two close family members likely contributed to the sensitive Lincoln's lifelong bouts of depression. His life became a mixture of grand accomplishments and personal loss.

Every school child in the US is familiar with the image of a young Lincoln crouched by a fireplace, reading dim pages. That formative habit started in Indiana. His sporadic education, common in frontier times, and the few lessons gleaned from school and relatives, transformed Lincoln into a book lover. Calling him a "voracious" reader would be an understatement. The future president often neglected work and even eating in favor of a good book. His stepmother, Sally, encouraged his reading and gave him access to her small collection of books.

It was in Indiana that his future ambitions solidified and sharpened. Here, he improved his skills as a public speaker, delighting family and friends with jokes and stories.

From a young age, Lincoln's religious upbringing vehemently opposed slavery, including his church in Indiana. Although his personal religious views remain cloudy, there is little doubt those views against slavery had a lasting effect. A flatboat trip from Indiana to New Orleans exposed a nineteen-year -old Lincoln to the full horrors of Southern slavery.

At twenty-one, Lincoln traveled with his family to Illinois, leaving behind his Indiana home and establishing himself in what would be his permanent home state. Illinois' claim is significant. It was there he practiced law, entered politics and, ultimately, won the White House.

But Indiana's claim is not insignificant. That characteristics most admired in Lincoln—his love of learning, his sense of civic duty, and his hatred of slavery—evolved in Indiana. Kentucky has his birth, Illinois has his body, but from 1816 to 1830 Indiana had shaped the legend.

Indiana: First and Last in Rotary Jails

By Zach Hoom

A Midwest experiment in the late 19th and early 20th centuries, the first, and last, rotary jail both have ties to Indiana. According to a patent filed in 1881, William H. Brown designed the first rotary jail, which was built by the Haugh, Ketcham & Co. iron foundry in Indianapolis.

The premise behind these interesting, if impractical, structures was simple: Prison cells rested on a rotating platform, with only one opening for the entire jail, the idea being that it would be easy to manage and impossible to escape from. As great as these

14

convict carousels may sound in theory, in practice they caused a lot of problems for inmates and prison staff alike.

Almost immediately, prison officials reported injuries, largely involving prisoners' limbs getting crushed by the rotating platform. These injuries and mechanical problems compounded, and most of the rotary jails ceased operation within a few years. These jails' cells were welded into a stationary position with individual doors.

By 1939, all of the rotary jails in the United States had been condemned, with the exception of the Pottawattamie County Jail in Council Bluffs, Iowa, which ceased operations in 1969.

There are no longer any prisoners housed in these jails, but Crawfordsville, Indiana, is home to the last fully-functional one. The Montgomery County Jail and Sheriff's Residence was built in 1882. No longer used to house inmates or the sheriff, the building now contains a local history and prison museum; in 1975, it was listed on the National Register of Historic Places.

If you're passing through Crawfordsville, the museum and jail are definitely worth checking out. If prison carousels and condemned 19th century jails aren't your thing, the building itself is located in the Crawfordsville Commercial Historic District, which is a neighborhood well worth a visit in its own right.

The Crawfordsville Commercial Historic District contains some wonderfully-preserved architecture from the 19th and early 20th century, including the Otto Schlemmer Building, which was built all the way back in 1854. Like the rotary jail, the Schlemmer building was added to the National Register of Historic Places in 1985, and the entire district joined the registry in 1992.

The First Theme Park: Santa Claus Land

By Zach Hoom

Theme parks are a uniquely 20th century invention.The first one didn't pop up in California, Chicago or Coney Island, but right here in Indiana in 1946.

In 1941, retired Evansville industrialist Louis J. Koch found himself in Santa Claus, Indiana. The father of 9 children himself, Mr. Koch wondered why there was no Santa Claus IN Santa Claus to entertain children—surely every child visiting the town must grow disappointed when Saint Nick never shows. A devoted family man, Koch took it upon himself to make sure that this

17

wouldn't happen. He set out to provide year-round access to Santa Claus for kids in Indiana and the Midwest.

World War II delayed the project, but construction commenced in 1945 and on August 3rd, 1946, Santa Claus Land opened to the public, becoming America's first theme park.

At first, the park was free to enter and consisted of Christmas theme toy displays, a toy shop, a restaurant, children's rides and Santa. Shortly afterwards, Bill Koch, Louis' son, assumed control of the park and added a number of attractions, including new rides, a second restaurant and even a deer farm.

In 1955, the park began charging adults 50 cents to enter, though children still visited for free. Attendance continued to grow. Future president Ronald Reagan even stopped by for a photo with Santa. With this added revenue, the park added numerous rides and attractions named after Santa's reindeer, some of which still exist today. The park also began incorporating live acts and children's choirs.

In 1960, Bill Koch married Patricia Yellig, whose father Jim was the park's Santa Claus. The couple had five children, including Will Koch, who ran the park for over twenty years.
In the mid-1970's, Santa Claus Land began courting adult and teenage visitors and added Americana-themed park rides in the years that followed. In 1984, Santa Claus Land, now under the presidency of Will Koch, was rebranded as Holiday World.

The park expanded, and added sections celebrating the Fourth of July and Halloween. In the early 1990's, the park added an adjacent water park and three wooden roller coasters, including *The Raven*, considered one of the most popular rollercoasters in the world.

Although it is now known as Holiday World & Splashin' Safari, and contains sections for Halloween, the Fourth of July, and Thanksgiving, guests still enter the park through the Christmas section, where Santa is waiting to welcome kids to Santa Claus, Indiana, as he has for over 70 years.

Indiana, the Birthplace of Professional Baseball

By Zach Hoom

Baseball occupies a unique place in the annals of American history and culture. Although it's an essential part of what makes America *American*, its history and origins remain contested. The specifics of the game's earliest days are a whole different story, with multiple cities, towns and states laying claim to their piece of baseball history.

Cooperstown, New York, brands itself as the birthplace of baseball. Hoboken, New Jersey, claims the first recorded game took place at its Elysian Fields.

In Indiana, we are unconcerned with this noise; historians know, with absolute certainty, that the first professional baseball game was played in Fort Wayne in 1871.

Though some teams began paying players in 1869, the first professional league was the National Association of Professional Base Ball Players, a precursor to today's National League. Founded in March of 1871, when representatives from 10 teams met above a saloon in New York City to iron out the details of the budding sport. Two of the teams balked at the "outlandish" ten dollar league fee, so only eight teams remained - the Philadelphia Athletics, New York Mutuals, Washington Olympics, Troy Haymakers, Chicago White Stockings, Rockford Forest Cities, Cleveland Forest Cities, and the Boston Red Stockings.

In the days following the meeting, a team from Fort Wayne would step forward, ten dollars in hand, and become the ninth.

The Fort Wayne Kekionga, named for a nearby Miami Indian settlement, had just added ace pitcher Bobby Matthews and a number of other talented players from a bankrupt Baltimore team. This Fort Wayne team hoped for redemption after a bad showing the last few years.

Redemption came, at least at first. The Kekionga hosted the first professional game in history in Fort Wayne and defeated the favored Cleveland Forest Cities 2-0 in front of 200 spectators at Kekionga Baseball Grounds.

The team sold season tickets for $5, but attendance was poor. Following their historic first win, the club lost steam and limped to the end of the season. Several players, including star pitcher Bobby Matthews, would go on to have respectable careers with other teams.

Although Fort Wayne hosted the first pro game, Indiana has never hosted a Major League Baseball team. Nonetheless, minor league teams like the Evansville Otters, the Fort Wayne Tin Caps, the Gary Southshore Railcats, the Indianapolis Indians, and the South Bend Silver Hawks keep Indiana's baseball culture strong.

Slabs of Stone

By Tim Bean

Limestone seems an odd thing to march out when humble-bragging about your home state, but it's no odder than the orange groves of Florida or the hardwood of Michigan. If I had pick of a natural resource to brag about, I'd rather it be hunks of fossilized marine life than a piece of fruit.

Indiana's limestone…is pretty awesome. Limestone grading relies on the purity of its calcium carbonate content. The higher the content percentage, the higher the quality. The limestone deposits of Central and South Central Indiana consistently provide some of the highest quality limestone in the world (generally above 97% calcium carbonate content).

Without delving into a geology lesson, Indiana limestone (also called *Bedford limestone* or *Salem limestone*) owes its quality to the receding shores of a 500-million-years-old lake that deposited the shells of single-celled creatures. Our limestone sprang from the remnants of an ancient reef. Time and pressure did the rest, resulting in limestone celebrated for its workability and strength.

The quarries of Bedford, Indiana, nicknamed the Limestone Capital of the World, have provided the limestone for many famous landmarks, like the Pentagon and the National Cathedral. The Empire Quarry in Bedford is by far the most famous. This now-defunct quarry's steep walls once provided the stone slabs used to construct the Empire State Building.

Bedford's residents hoped the reputation of its quality limestone would turn the city into a thriving tourist destination. Planners decided to construct a replica limestone pyramid, one-fifth the size of the Great Pyramid of Giza, along with a replica of the Great Wall of China. The US government liked the idea and handed over $500,000 for the project.

The city put down a single layer of limestone bricks for the pyramid before the government changed its mind, revoked the funds, and left one of Indiana's strangest monuments: the Bedford Limestone Pyramid, which is simply a massive square of limestone bricks.

The site is on private property, and I can't officially recommend you check it out. Whatever you do, *don't* drive 15 miles south of Bloomington, *don't* turn south on Old Highway 37 until you reach a metal fence near its dead end, and *don't* hop the fence on foot to see the sprawling one-layer pyramid.

(Wink).

Gradually, Indiana limestone became a niche building material, because of the high cost involved in mining, shaping and transporting the stone. Acid rain also took its toll on limestone market, with industrial pollutants pitting tiny holes in the stone and gradually wearing it away.

Today, the largest limestone producer in the state, the Indiana Limestone Company, offers a variety of limestone products for construction or decoration. Even if you're not in the market for limestone, consider browsing their website for the sake of curiosity. They've got excellent drone video of their quarries. Put the video on full-screen, lean your face closer to your screen and get set to get queasy as its flies over the limestone abysses.

Indy's Museum of Psychphonics

By Tim Bean

Did you know Indianapolis possesses the highest concentration of funkalicious musicality in the entire Midwest? In fact, the only place funkier in the entire world at any given time is the ten feet surrounding Mister George Clinton, King of Funk. Where in Indy can you locate this nexus of nastiness, this gathering of groovalicious funkadelia?

To be honest, it can't be found right now. It temporarily closed in July of 2017. But when it reopens later this year, you'll find musical Mecca at the Museum of Psychphonics.

The museum is a sensory saturation of American weirdness, dedicated to the secret streak of strangeness that we rarely bring

26

out in polite company. It's an ode to the part of you that sings in the shower or jiggles your hips when you pop in the earbuds.

You know *exactly* what I'm talking about.

Originally tucked away in a 100-square foot room of Indy's hipster-haven, Joyful Noise Recordings, the Museum of Psychphonics will soon be reopening in a (slightly) larger venue in Fountain Square.

Featured funky exhibitions are as mysterious and bizarre; both staff and visitors are strongly encouraged not to share the specifics of a visit to the Museum of Psychphonics, only the broad-stroke emotions. Not what you see, but what you feel. Actual exhibits are hush-hush. Open mouths are discouraged; open minds are necessary.

I'll share one, since it's already had a little local press. It's a UFO. Not a UFO, exactly. A Mothership. And not really a Mothership, exactly, but a model of a Mothership. And not just a Mothership. It is the MOTHERSHIP.

The Parliament Funkadelic featured this small Mothership model in the 1970s in concert, just before Dr. Funkenstein, George Clinton's alter-ego, emerged from the larger Mothership backdrop onstage. Any fans of P-Funk will be in awe. It's an artifact of modern music, demarcating the line between funk and Funk.

'A Christmas Story': Nostalgia, Ad Nauseam

By Tim Bean

I thought I loved the holiday film *A Christmas Story*. After a visit to Cleveland a few years ago, I discovered some people LOVE the film.

Hoosiers are equal parts amazed and insulted to learn that he most famous film features Northwest Indiana wasn't filmed in

Northwest Indiana, but in a suburb of Cleveland during the film's production. The film's producers had good reason.

Hammond of the 1980s did not look like Hammond of the 1940s. The quaint suburbs had vanished and the city had become crowded with commerce and industry. Searching far and wide in the Midwest, the producers discovered a small suburb of Cleveland that you'd swear was one of the narrow, twisting streets off Hammond's Calumet Avenue, circa 1948.

Last year, on a pilgrimage to the Rock and Roll Hall of Fame, friends asked if I wanted to visit Ralphie's house. I watched the film every holiday season, had once dreamed of owning a BB gun, and knew the thrill of receiving that ONE Christmas present you wanted so badly you dreamed about it (for me, it was the 1989 Game Boy).

It wasn't easy to find. Without GPS, most visitors would lose their way through the sadistically-designed streets of Cleveland's residential neighborhoods, compounded by residential parking clogging the street itself. This made for some claustrophobic navigation. After finally finding the house, we spent another ten minutes finding parking, reluctantly parking in a resident's yard featuring a sign reading PARKING $20 (later on, we learned the *Story* house had free parking, but we never saw it). We reluctantly paid the extortion and then walked a block up to the *A Christmas Story* house, which was a renovated Craftsman-style house from the 1920s or 30s, complete with the monolithic porch pillars.

Not a pretty house, but a familiar one. It was a house I had seen fifty times growing up, although always covered with snow instead of July's sunshine. The museum had recently completed a massive renovation of the house, and I recognized the time and care put into recreating the movie memory. But an ugly house is still an ugly house. But shining oh-so-brightly in the front window was the Leg Lamp.

Tickets came first. We jogged across the street to the gift shop to purchase tickets at $11 a pop. The gift shop was wall-to-wall nostalgia. Anything and everything that had to do with the house (along with *National Lampoon's Christmas Vacation*) was for sale. This included a collectible Christmas village from *Story*, Lifebuoy soap to suck on, a box of F-F-ffudge, replica leg lamps, and the official Daisy Red Ryder BB gun.

I bought a soda.

My friends bought trinkets and ornaments, as did most visitors. While I stood in line to buy my ticket and a Coke, I watched the person ahead of me drop several hundred dollars on homes and figures for the Christmas village. That's a little weird.

A small museum attached to the gift shop contained items used in the filming, most of which I didn't recognize. I strolled through the museum in about twenty minutes, but most took much longer, pouring over every item like the IRS over Capone's cooked books.

I spent the entire tour people-watching. They bounced from item to item and I witnessed the pattern of the nostalgically obsessed: ogle the item, patiently read the informative display, ogle the item again with fervor, make an approving comment or grunt, and then move to the next item.

The house was small, but all houses of that era seem small inside. Everything, from the wallpaper to the wood trim, gleamed immaculately. After two dozen people collected in the crowded living room, the tour guide started her spiel, speaking for twenty minutes before we moved to another room. I don't remember any of it. I DO remember being hot and uncomfortable in a room of sweaty strangers.

The house tour consisted of mostly *Did you know...* moments punctuated by our guide's gestures at a window or a door to indicate filming locations. The backyard was there, and visitors could stand whereto on-camera Ralphie stood as he fending off robbers with chewing tobacco, spurs and his trusty Red Ryder BB

Gun. I found the willingness of visitors to stand in line for the honor of looking out of the window the most interesting part of the visit. That and discovering a massive wasp nest in the 'Story' house's shed—I'm allergic.

If you love the film, it's worth seeing if you're in Cleveland, but not worth a special trip. Of course, if you LOVE the film, and this article irritated you, then you won't shy at spending the extra dough.

My nostalgia for the film has abated with my life's mileage, but I still appreciate the characters, atmosphere and, most of all, the narrative skill of author Jean Shepard. The man wielded descriptive nostalgia like an anti-aircraft gun.

Honestly, if Jean Shepard were still around and went to visit Ralphie's house from *A Christmas Story* I think he'd find himself doing more people-watching than anything else as well.

The Midwest's First Long-Distance Auto Race

The Chicago Automobile Clubs Grand Stand, Viaduct in distance. Press and Judges stand. The start and finish of the two great races, Indiana Trophy and Cobe Cup.

By Mary Giorgio

In 1909, one of the first long-distance races in the Midwest took place in Crown Point, Indiana. Billed as the "Vanderbilt of the West" (the famed Vanderbilt Cup Race in New York began in 1904), the race sought to live up to the grandeur of its eastern counterpart.

In 1909, automobiles were still fairly new, and many people didn't own one. The race was a novelty for many Hoosiers who emerged from their homes to witness the strange sight.

The Crown Point race was sponsored by Ira M. Cobe of the Chicago Motor Club. The race ran along rural highways from

33

Crown Point to Lowell to Cedar Lake and back, beginning and ending at the intersection of Indiana Avenue and Burrell. Dr. Cobe billed his competition as the "ultimate endurance race."

AUTOMOBILE RACES
J·U N E 18 - 19, 1909

We have by far the best location and point of view on the whole course at Mr. Lew Chapman's premises on North Clark street, Lowell, Indiana Only two blocks north of Lowell National Bank, and three blocks from Monon depot on a high embankment, where there will be no possible danger of racing machines running into stand and where racers can be seen for Two Miles on the fastest piece of road on the course. You will have no trouble to go and come from stand at any time during race.

WESTERN STOCK CHASSIS RACE *for the* COBE TROPHY JUNE 18-19

Zartman's Busses

and other conveyances will meet all trains on the

C. I. & S. Ry.
AT NORTH HAYDEN

to convey you to Lowell and the grandstand .

Refreshments on Ground

Schma''s Hotel is the place to eat; only short distance from stand.

Grandstand Tickets $2.00 per day
FOR FURTHER INFORMATION OR RESERVED SEAT TICKETS ADDRESS
Lowell Grandstand Co.,
Lowell, Indiana
Tickets also on sale at Schmal's Hotel
Reference—Lowell National Bank

In preparation for the event, Cobe built huge grandstands for the anticipated audience. Telegraph stations were constructed along the race route to relay standings. Pedestrian bridges were built over the route. Roads were treated with a "taroid," a mixture of oil and tar that helped the vehicles travel faster. It was an expensive undertaking, so Cobe charged spectators a $2 admission fee to enter the grandstands.

Two competitions made up the event. The first took place on Friday, June 18, with 16 racers competing in the Indiana Trophy Race. Some of the country's most daring drivers turned up for the competition, including Harry Stutz of Bearcat fame. Racers traveled 232.74 miles from Crown Point to Lowell and back. Joe Matson took first place in a Chalmers-Detroit Blue Bird.

On Saturday, June 19, the much-anticipated Cobe Trophy Race took place. Twelve racers sped off from Crown Point in an epic 8-hour, 395.6 mile race. The first racer to cross the finish line was Billy Bourque, but he was not the winner. Start times had been staggered for logistical reasons, so the race's winner was actually the second car to complete the course, Louis Chevrolet.

Chevrolet's souped-up Buick had beaten Bourque by just over a minute, averaging 49.287 mph, with a winning time of 8 hours, 1 minute, and 30 seconds. More astounding is that Chevrolet's time included repair of a blown cylinder earlier in the race.

The Indianapolis Motor Speedway was founded later that year, and Chevrolet would go on to win nine IndyCar races. In 1911, he founded Chevrolet motor company, which capitalized on his celebrity as a champion racer.

For Crown Point, Cobe's 1909 racing competition was the only organized automobile race to take place in the city. The event had been a failure from a revenue standpoint, with nearly $25,000 in losses. The race was too long for most spectators and many who did come to see the epic competition discovered they could avoid the $2 admission fee by watching from unmanned portions of the extensive rural route.

In 1910, the Cobe Race was held at the newly opened Indianapolis Motor Speedway. By 1911, the Speedway had begun its Indy500 series, and the Cobe Race was discontinued. Today, few people remember the epic car race that took place a century ago in Crown Point, Lowell, and Cedar Lake. Nevertheless, the competition was an important part of early automobile racing history.

The original Cobe Trophy is now owned and on display in the Indianapolis Motor Speedway Museum.

Three Girls Gone: the Ford Pinto and Indiana v. Ford Motor Co.

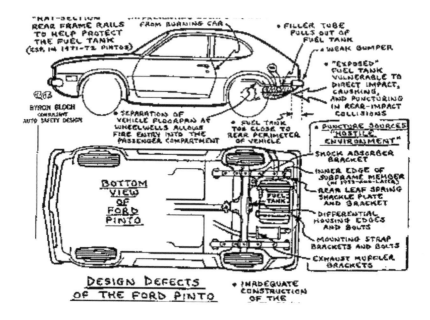

By Tim Bean

*Author's note: Although I had no difficulties in uncovering details of the Ford Pinto's rise and fall, it took much longer to find the names of the three Hoosier girls who perished in the 1978 accident. That's not right. I hope their family knows people still care.

August 10th, 1978. Goshen, Indiana.

On their way to a church volleyball practice, the three teenage girls—sisters Lyn and Judy Ulrich, and their cousin Donna Ulrich—chugged along U.S. 33 in a dusty 1973 Ford Pinto.

After a quick stop at a filling station, driver Judy Ulrich glanced at her rearview mirror and noticed the gas cap cover yawning wide open. She remembered leaving the gas cap on the car's trunk, but not putting it back. She flicked on her hazard lights and nudged the car to the shoulder, hoping that the gas cap hadn't tumbled off the trunk yet.

Behind them, 21-year-old Richard Dugger attempted to light a cigarette as he cruised along 33 in a two-ton van. He pursed his lips, bringing the lighter close, but he fumbled with the cigarette and it fell onto the van floor. He leaned down awkwardly, his eyes darting from the road to the floor mat. His left hand remained on the steering wheel, while his right feverishly groped for the cigarette. It only took seconds for his fingers to close around it, but when he sat up, it was too late.

The Ford Pinto that had been a safe distance ahead now filled his entire windshield, its yellow flashers glaring. He stomped the brake pedal automatically but barely slowed.

Lyn Ulrich   Judy Ulrich   Donna Ulrich

The 4,000 pound van tore into the rear of the Pinto, hitting it like a flying anvil. The subcompact car's rear end crumpled in a spray of metal and gasoline. The entire Pinto lurched into the air and landed askew, with one tire in the weeds and the other on the road.

Duggar kicked his door open and jumped onto the road, his shoes crunching over broken glass, and called out to the Pinto's passengers. He saw the three girls inside.

Duggar could taste the slick gas on his tongue. It permeated the air.

He called out. "Hey! Are you—"

The cloud of gas vapor surrounding the Pinto exploded with a flat WHAPP!, transforming the car into a cauldron of fire, glass, and metal. Dugger staggered back. He pasted his arm over his face against the wall of heat, squinting at the flames. Horrified, he watched the three dark outlines lurching from side to side behind the cracked glass. They pounded their fists uselessly against the crumpled Pinto doors, now welded tightly closed with the impact.

He couldn't get closer. There was nothing he could do to help the girls trapped inside. Dugger took a few weak steps before falling to his knees well behind the car. The heat now singed his hair and clothes. Richard Duggar could only listen and weep at the side of the Indiana highway on that August evening.

The coroner reported Donna and Lyn Ulrich died within seconds inside the burning Pinto. Judy succumbed to her injuries at a nearby hospital the next day, just after recounting the accident to police.

Six months later after the girls' deaths, Mattie Ulrich, Judy and Lyn's mother, received a notice from the Ford Motor Company: a design flaw in the fuel system rendered their 1973 Ford Pinto prone to gas tank explosions. Especially in rear-end collisions.

The Ford Pinto: The Little Carefree Car

In 1968, Lee Iacocca, legendary automotive innovator and then-president of Ford Motor Company, demanded two things from the company's new subcompact, later named the Ford Pinto: it would weigh less than one ton and cost less than $2,000 dollars.

These were bold demands. Ford had not made vehicles that light since 1907. And $2,000 for a brand new car? Ford designers threw themselves into the task, prioritizing cost far above safety concerns and adhering to Iacocca's famous—now infamous—quote "Safety doesn't sell."

Ford designers and engineers managed to design, build, test, and deliver this revolutionary Ford model in just over two years, half the average time for a design-to-delivery timeline for a new American auto model. Iacocca didn't recognize this as efficiency as much as necessity: the current popularity of foreign subcompact cars like the Volkswagen Beetle and Datsun Bluebird had left US automakers in the dust. Ford discovered both AMC and GM had subcompact models in development (the AMC Gremlin and Chevrolet Vega) and refused to fall behind. Iacocca micromanaged the project (nicknamed "Lee's Car") obsessively to ensure the Pinto would reach the American market in record time. It did.

On September 11th, 1970, Ford introduced the Pinto to the public as a "carefree" alternative to the lumbering and expensive American autos of its day. The Pinto's style and design was uniquely European, with a peppy four-cylinder engine, rear-wheel drive, and bucket seats. The basic model cost $1,850 (approx. $11,000 in 2019), comfortably under Iacocca's price point, and it weighed only 2,015 pounds, a featherweight in American autos.

Within four months, Ford sold over 100,000 Pintos, and it became one of the company's best-selling cars, dominating the domestic subcompact market. During the model's entire run, from 1971 to 1980, Ford sold over 3.1 million Pintos. By any reckoning, "Lee's Car" was a success.

"Safety Doesn't Sell"

The Pinto's most egregious design flaw resided in the the fuel tank placement. Ford designers nestled it between the rear axle and flimsy rear bumper, almost guaranteeing any slow-speed fender bender could result in a tank rupture. The filler neck, traveling from beneath the gas cap to the gas tank tore easily, rending a nearly two-inch hole in the sheet metal and sloshing volatile fuel beneath the car. Surrounding the gas tank were a half dozen puncture points in the guise of bolts.

The spacious rear of the Ford Pinto came at a cost as well. In a rear end collision, the empty space caused the entire back third of the car to crumple, wedging the body and frame tightly against the car doors, making them virtually impossible to open. And if there was a fire, gaps in the Pinto's floor allowed flames to quickly reach up into the car's passenger compartment.

The solution? Roughly $10-15 worth of parts and labor per Pinto.

Iacocca's demands had created a very dangerous automobile, then left it on the market for nearly a decade. And the "Pinto Memo" proved Ford knew it as early as 1973.

The "Pinto Memo": The Unkindest Math of All

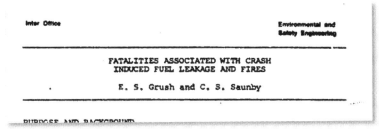

In 1973, Ford's Environmental and Safety Engineering Department released an inter-office memo entitled "Fatalities

Induced Fuel Leakage and Fires" to share the company's efforts to block new fuel system requirements. Later known as "The Pinto Memo," this communication included ALL passenger cars and light trucks in its calculations, and introduced the term *cost-benefit analysis* into the public arena.

Authors E.S. Grush and C.S. Saunby (supported by Ford engineers J.D. Hromi and R.B. MacLean) estimated that recalling and modifying ALL current passenger cars and light trucks to meet proposed NHTSA (National Highway Traffic Safety Administration) fuel-system regulations would cost approximately $11 per vehicle, for a total cost of $137 million. A hefty sum, even if shared by all American automakers.

But what if they just didn't do it? Grush and Saunby estimated the projected costs of litigation and settlements if safety improvements were not implemented (ascribing a value of $200,000 to a human life) and predicted a total cost of $50 million. Their conclusion is as clear as it is cold, and the memo ended with this unambiguous position: "...the implementation costs far outweigh the expected benefits."

To paraphrase (only very slightly), it was more cost-effective for the auto industry to forgo fuel safety improvements and let passengers burn.

Indiana v. Ford Motor Co.

Elkhart County prosecutors, armed with the "Pinto Memo" and the tragedy of the Ulrich girls, went after Ford Motor Company, but not in civil court. They leveled three counts of reckless homicide against Ford Motor Company in *Indiana v. Ford Motor Co*, putting the entire company in criminal court. It was a first for Ford Motors and the entire nation.

While the Elkhart County prosecutors worked with a minuscule budget ($20,000) and a legal lineup composed mostly of volunteers, Ford Motors spared no expense.

They hired one of the nation's top trial lawyers, James F. Neal, to spearhead Ford's defense. Neal soared into court with a million dollar budget and a staff of eighty professionals. Ford had wealth, experience, and legal precedence on their side. What they did not have was public sentiment.

Make no mistake: Ford Motor Company was scared to death. A corporate entity cannot logistically face jail time, and the maximum fine for reckless homicide in Indiana in 1978 was $80,000, a fraction of the defense's budget. But if found guilty, the legal precedent would forever alter corporate America, bringing product liability law, and negligence, into the arena of criminal law. American companies would answer to federal regulations in both civil and criminal settings. The executives of one of America's largest companies foresaw a dismal future with their heads on chopping blocks. Even in the best circumstances, *Indiana v. Ford Motor Co.* had the potential to bind corporate America in a straitjacket of red tape.

A Landmark Case

James Neal's strategy wasn't to directly defend the Pinto, or even dwell on the Ulrich girls or Dugger's liability. Instead, Neal focused on two issues: first, the impropriety of bringing a civil case into a criminal court; second, the Pinto itself was no more dangerous than any other American subcompact on the road in the late 1970s. Ford's case relied on the logical fallacy *tu quoque*-- an appeal to hypocrisy, two wrong do not make a right, or, in simpler terms, "They're doing it so why can't I?".

The outcome came as no surprise. Elkhart County prosecutors fought their hardest, but outgunning Ford's legal dreadnought was a battle lost before begun. Ford was found not guilty to the delight of its legal team, executives, and stockholders. In 1980, the company magnanimously agreed to a token settlement of $7500 for each of the Ulrich girls, paying the small sum to a family that no doubt simply wanted to put the travesty behind them.

No Concluding the Controversy

Ford Motor Company won the case, but it never completely regained the trust of the American people. Its hearty but heartless defense in *Indiana v. Ford Motor Co.*, and the irrefutable contents of the "Pinto Memo," portrayed the entire American automotive industry as a soulless engine of greed and profit, betraying its image as the lifeblood of America. It took decades for Ford to repair the damage. To this day, Ford has never again enjoyed its trusted status of the 50s and 60s.

Ford initiated a "voluntary recall" of the Ford Pinto soon after the trial. The public saw this as both an admission of guilt and an effort to prevent further lawsuits. Sales of the Ford Pinto had slowed but not slumped, but Ford executives decided the best strategy was to distance itself from "Lee's Car." 1980 marked the last year of Pinto manufacture.

Even today, the case remains controversial. Ford defenders decry the case as a parade of media bias, villainization, and legal overstepping. Detractors insist the case demonstrates willful negligence, with the trial's outcome resulting from cash resources, not righteousness. It is a heated argument and one that resonates now more than ever.

That's all trivial now to the three Ulrich girls. Media wars, settlements, legal precedence, and safety inspections don't mean anything now. The entire auto industry could collapse, and it wouldn't matter. Those frivolous things ended on an Indiana highway in 1978. There's only the memories of their short but happy lives in the minds of their family and friends.

Mediums in the Midwest: the American Spiritualism Movement

INTERIOR OF GARDEN OF PRAYER
CAMP CHESTERFIELD, CHESTERFIELD, INDIA

By Mary Giorgio

In 1848, a strange phenomenon took hold across America. Claiming that they could communicate with the dead, Margaret and Catherine Fox toured the country demonstrating their methods. Strange knocking or rapping sounds in reply to their attempts to reach the spirits were widely seen as proof that such communication was possible. The Modern American Spiritualism Movement was born.

Indiana and the Midwest were no exceptions to the national enthusiasm for the movement. Spiritualist societies popped up across the Hoosier state. Such was the momentum behind the movement that it was more than 100 years before interest significantly waned.

Indiana's champion of spiritualism was John Westerfield of Anderson. Westerfield began arranging for speakers on topics of mesmerism and clairvoyance in the 1840s to lecture at Anderson's Union Hall. Following the death of his young son in 1855, Westerfield was drawn further into the spiritualist movement. He and his wife began to host seances to communicate with their dead son. Their experiences led them to become deeply involved in the Spiritualist movement.

By the early 1880s, the spiritualism movement had become so popular across America that spiritualist camps began to open as gathering places for like-minded spiritualists and their followers. The Westerfields visited one of these camps in 1883. They were so inspired by Frazier's Grove, Michigan, that when they returned home, they began making plans for a similar establishment in Indiana.

In 1886, Westerfield formed the Indiana Association of Spiritualists, a group that has remained active for more than 130 years. In 1891, the association purchased land along the banks of the White River in Chesterfield, Indiana. There, they created Camp Chesterfield. Initially, the camp was rustic, with simple tents and summer cabins.

Soon, a shared dining hall, auditorium, séance cabins, and lodging house were built. Newer buildings replaced these early

48

WESTERN HOTEL — CAMP CHESTERFIELD. THE INDIANA ASSOCIATION OF SPIRITUALISTS, CHESTERFIELD, INDIANA

structures in the 1910s. Construction of new buildings continued post-World War II. The last structure, an art gallery, opened in 1958. By then, interest in the movement had substantially decreased and the camp's attendance dropped significantly.

The camp was not without controversy in its heyday. In 1925, the quiet camp was hit with scandal when 14 of its mediums were arrested for operating under false pretenses. Charges were later dropped. In July of 1960, the *Psychic Observer* published an expose revealing that two filmed seances were hoaxes. In 1976, former camp medium M. Lamar Keene published his memoir, in which he admitted to defrauding customers.

The camp survived these allegations and continues to operate today. The camp is open to the public. Visitors can explore the grounds or make an appointment for a reading with a medium.

In 2002, Camp Chesterfield was designated as a historic district and listed on the National Register of Historic Places for its significance as one of the last few spiritualist camps that were so popular in the United States at the start of the twentieth century.

Before the Detroit Pistons, We Had the Fort Wayne-Zollner Pistons

By Mary Giorgio

It's no secret that the Hoosier state has had a long love affair with basketball. In the 1940s, Fort Wayne, Indiana, was home to the state's first professional basketball team. The Fort Wayne Zollner Pistons delighted fans for 15 years before relocating to a larger market in Detroit.

The Zollner Pistons were founded in 1941 by Fred Zollner. Along with his sister, Janet, Fred owned Zollner Corporation, a local foundry that manufactured pistons for cars, trucks, and locomotives.

In the team's early years, money was scarce and professional basketball players did not command the salaries that they earn today. Zollner paid his players a share of profits at the end of each season, amounting to around $2,500 a year. To make ends meet, players were employed in Zollner's factory.

The team was forced to play its home games at the North Side High School gym. In 1952, they were able to secure a space at the Allen County War Memorial Coliseum.

From the beginning, the Zollner Pistons were a competitive team. As part of the National Basketball League's (NBL) Central Division, the Pistons won the league championship in 1944 and 1945. They won the world professional basketball tournament in 1944, 1945, and 1946. In 1948, Zollner changed the team's name to the Fort Wayne Pistons.

During their years in Fort Wayne, the Pistons were at the forefront of innovation in the rules of the basketball game. In the late 1940s, they successfully experimented with an enlarged foul line (12 feet instead of the former 6) at three consecutive games. In the early 1950s, the 24-second shot clock was instituted in response to an epic bout of shot-stalling that took place in a game against the Minnesota Lakers.

Zollner became a prominent figure in American basketball. In 1949, he convened officials from NBL and National Basketball Association (NBA) in his Fort Wayne home to discuss a possible merger. It is said that the merger took place at Zollner's kitchen table.

This led to the development of a stronger and wealthier league. More games were played during each season, and players began to command higher salaries. The Pistons star player, George Yardley, made $15,000 a year in the 1950s.

After the merger, Zollner began to realize that Fort Wayne was not a large enough city to support the new league structure. There weren't enough fans to fill the stands and generate the revenue needed to sustain the team.

In 1957, he announced his decision to relocate the team to Detroit, Michigan. He hoped that the larger city would result in a larger fan base and more profitable franchise. Zollner remained the owner of the Pistons until 1974, when he sold the team to Bill Davidson.

Business Outside, Opulent Inside: the Evansville Victory Theatre

By Mary Giorgio

In the 1920s, Americans obsessed over movies.

The first true motion pictures were produced in the late 1800s, and from the beginning, the American population was hooked. By the 1920s, movies had become so popular that it was not uncommon for small towns across the country to support two or three theaters. The same held true in Indiana, where theaters sprung up even in the smallest communities.

In Evansville, the opulent Victory Theatre opened its doors in 1921. In anticipation of its great popularity, the theater accommodated a whopping 2,500 people. It was said to be one of the largest theaters in the Midwest. On the upper floors of the building, the Sonntag Hotel offered out-of-towners an equally luxurious place to sleep.

The building was designed by Chicago architect John Pridemore. While its exterior is a plain 1920's commercial design, the interior was filled with opulent patriotic decor in blue and gold. The decor, like many similarly designed theaters across small-town America, was so ornate that the theater was often referred to as a palace. Constructed on the heels of World War I, the interior commemorated the Great War. The building even had air conditioning!

The idea for the theater and hotel came from stockholders of the American Trust and Savings Bank. They saw the presence of a theater and upscale hotel in Evansville as a lucrative proposition. Marcus Sonntag led the group's efforts to complete the project.

In the 1920s, the theater featured a daily program consisting of a Vaudeville act, movie, comedy routine, organ music, and a performance by a 10-piece orchestra. The variety of acts literally offered something for everyone. By 1926, however, American Trust and Savings Bank decided to relinquish management of the theater facility to Loews Theatres. The building thereafter became known as Loews Theatre.

In 1928, the theater featured Evansville's first talking picture, an epic tale titled *Tenderloin*. Later that year, Loews became the first theater to run a stand-alone talkie show in Evansville, *The Jazz Singer*, featuring Al Jolson.

In the ensuing decades, the theater's popularity dwindled as newer, more modern facilities appeared in Evansville. Loews Theatre closed in 1971. It was divided into a triplex for a few years, before permanently closing in 1979.

In 1998, the City of Evansville began restoring the theater building to its original glory. The facility is co-managed with the Ford Center Arena and hosts a variety of performances each year. The Victory Theatre is now home to the Evansville Philharmonic Orchestra. It also hosts local ballet and modern dance companies, a theater company, and a tour company.

Today, the Victory Theatre is one of the remaining examples of the opulent movie palaces so popular in the 1920s. Americans' obsession with extravagant European style decor faded as the century wore on. Eventually, many older theaters were torn down. The Victory Theatre is listed on the National Register of

Historic Places, a testament to the theater's enduring legacy in the history of Hoosiers' favorite pastimes.

Indiana's Mysterious and Marvelous Toy Fairy

By Tim Bean

To protect the identity of this kind-hearted "Summer Santa," portions of this article have been redacted, including her name and location. She'd prefer to remain anonymous, and while I'll share her story, I won't spoil her fun. Happy flying!

Her name is [**redacted**] and she flies through the air with the greatest of ease...but she's not available for parties.

A generous yet mysterious paramotor (a powered paraglider) has spent several summers piloting the smooth skies over [**redacted**] and dropping armloads of toys to surprised children for miles around. She's become such a familiar sight in [**redacted**] that hordes of children have begged their parents to "Follow that Toy Fairy!"

Long before [**redacted**] became the Toy Fairy, her paramotor was a familiar site in the rural suburbs of [**redacted**]. The paramotor's hefty, healthy buzz and rainbow colors flew in lazy, elegant circles safety above the tree tops and power lines. Sometimes [**redacted**] dipped low enough to raise an eyebrow, but no one doubted her deft handling of the aircraft. She quickly became a familiar site every [**redacted**] summer.

Then she got creative. This mysterious and marvelous flyer began dropping soft (and safe) toys to children for the last two summers. Sometimes they receive an armful of plush toys, sometimes a couple footballs, but [**redacted**] always does it with a wink, a wave, and at a safe distance. She's also been known to shave a few treetops when she spots a festive party below.

Appreciative parents have called her a "hero" and a "rock star," but any attempt to contact her directly has always been politely brushed away. Even the local radio station [**redacted**] and newspaper [**redacted**] have found no luck getting her story, simply because she's not interested in the attention.

Parents have flocked to [**redacted**], posting heartfelt thanks and pictures of their beaming children showing off their new toys. But [**redacted**] just wants to stay a silent, anonymous Toy Fairy.

Summer's coming to an end, so if you're near [**redacted**], keep a watch on the skies, at least for a few more weeks. You may just spot her. For those that would like to thank [**redacted**] directly, don't bother with Facebook or Twitter...just give her a simple wave when she passes overhead.

The 1910 Kingsland Wreck: Indiana's Worst Interurban Train Disaster

By Mary Giorgio

In the early 1900s, before the days of widespread automobile ownership, residents of Indiana traveled from place to place by way of an intricately-connected system of interurban rail lines. Hundreds of interurban lines crossed the state, connecting cities and towns. While the system was an efficient way to travel quickly, accidents were common.

On September 21, 1910, Indiana experienced the worst inter-urban crash in American history. The crash occurred on the Fort Wayne and Wabash Valley Traction Line near Kingsland,

Indiana. The annual Fort Wayne Fair was in full swing, and extra trips had been added to the train schedule that day. A full load of people embarked at Bluffton. John Boyd, a survivor of the impending crash, would later recount the train was so full he had to stand on its rear stairs to catch a ride.

The interurban train was traveling around 40 mph. It had reached a point about six miles north of Bluffton when disaster struck. The northbound train rounded a curve and found itself directly in the path of a southbound train. Mr. Boyd later recalled the terror he felt when he realized the collision was inevitable. He jumped to safety mere seconds before the two trains collided.

It was not uncommon for northbound and southbound trains to share a track. A dispatcher was charged with monitoring train positions and notifying motormen of oncoming traffic. One train would then be instructed to pull into the side lane to allow the oncoming train to pass. Unfortunately, dispatchers could not communicate with trains when they were in motion in those days.

As a result, the dispatcher on duty that day was powerless to prevent the disaster.

Investigators would later question why, in those critical moments leading up to the crash, neither motorman had attempted to switch tracks or hit the brakes. The motormen claimed to have been so overcome with fear that neither had thought to act.

When the collision occurred, the southbound train was empty save for its crew. Because of its lighter weight, the southbound train flew up over the top of the northbound train, ripping the roof off the passenger car and settling on the bodies of the northbound train's riders. Of the approximately 50 people on board, 41 died. Over half of the passengers were from Bluffton. Mr. Boyd could never forget the eerie silence in the wake of the crash...followed by the weak cries of the wounded and dying.

In the immediate aftermath of the disaster, one of the conductors from the southbound train realized yet another train was speeding unaware towards the wreckage. Although injured, E. A. Spiller managed to walk ahead on the tracks, flag down the oncoming train, and prevent the unimaginable tragedy of another collision.

The residents of Bluffton buried the dead and continued with their lives. The company that owned both interurban lines, Wabash Valley Traction Company, lost many riders immediately following the crash. The company was eventually sold at auction. Despite the scale of the tragedy, the popularity of interurbans quickly rebounded and continued well into the late-1920s.

What is the Kokomo Hum?

By Tim Bean

Known simply as "the Hum" to Kokomo residents, this phenomena has plagued the "City of Firsts" since 1999, when reports of an endless, barely-audible monotonous Hum began trickling in. And not just in Kokomo.

Hundreds of cities across the country began reporting a similar rumble, described by sufferers as a large engine idling in the distance, or the rush of an underground river, or the inner ear's drone when covering one's ears (the flesh of your hands filters out high-pitched ambient noise, leaving only low-pitched sound).

The variety of similes used to describe the Hum aside, sufferers all agreed it was persistent and low-pitched (around 20 Hz). Quiet, but audible enough to cause discomfort, headaches, and, in some cases, vomiting and migraines. Despite the very visible effects of this phenomena, audiologists have been unable to reach a consensus on the source of the Hum, or if it even exists in the first place.

Maybe Mass Hysteria?

When contacted two decades ago, researchers considered mass hysteria the most likely cause of the Kokomo Hum. Mass hysteria is common, well-documented, and very contagious. During the Dancing Plague of 1518, 400 people uncontrollably danced for a days at a stretch. Dozens of people eventually died from malnutrition, exhaustion, and cardiac trauma. From dancing.

In the mid-1940s, the Mad Gasser of Mattoon (Illinois) hysteria caused citizens to become violently ill after choking on imagined odors in their homes. Conducting an exhaustive search, Mattoon

police found no trace of a "Mad Gasser" and dismissed it as mass hysteria.

Probably the most infamous case of hysteria for Hoosiers was the 1978 tragedy at Jonestown, in which a drug-addled and delusion Jim Jones brainwashed nearly a thousand followers, including many from the Indianapolis area, and coerced them into committing mass suicide. It was the largest loss of American civilian lives until 9/11 in 2001.

The Kokomo Hum, however, cannot be so easily dismissed, because possible causes and the effects of infrasound (extreme low-frequency) are indisputable. Studies on the physical effects of infrasound—sound waves at or below 20 Hz—on humans have shown effects ranging from feelings of dread or fear to insomnia to gastrointestinal stress to violent nausea. This typically depends on the subject's hearing acuity; not everyone can hear such a low-frequency noise.

Serious and Disciplined Study

At the forefront of this mystery is Dr. Glen MacPherson, whose hard work and rigid adherence to scientific standards have kept the Hum from falling into the trash bin of pseudoscience. Dr. MacPherson, former lecturer at the University of British Columbia, mathematics educator, ethnographic researcher, and curriculum advisor for UBC's Robson Campus, is the real deal.

After first hearing the Hum in 2012 in Canada, he discovered no database existed to collected data of the phenomena. He quickly established the World Hum Map and Database Project, which utilizes strict self-reporting to catalog Hum experiences around the world. A daunting task, Dr. MacPherson does his best with the site's self-reported data to an admirable degree. Self-reporting is a notoriously difficult method of data collection (it can often be misleading, incomplete, or inconclusive).

The World Hum database warns visitors clearly: "This is a place for disciplined inquiry, and not for wild speculation and conspiracy. There are many entertaining and interesting websites available for those who want to indulge in those activities."

Because of his efforts, greater numbers of professional audiologists have taken an interest in the Hum, although he still has detractors. Dr Jonathan Hazell, head researcher for the United Kingdom's Royal National Institute for Deaf People, didn't mince words when asked about the Hum: "Rubbish. Everybody who has tinnitus complains at first of environmental noise. 'Hummers' are a group of people who cannot accept that they have tinnitus."

Dr. MacPherson didn't dismiss the phenomena so readily.

Dr. MacPherson's Hypotheses

To be sure, Dr. MacPherson's evidence isn't refined enough to produce a definitive conclusion concerning the Hum phenomena in his native Canada, in Europe, or in Kokomo, Indiana. It does allow some educated guesses that may guide more comprehensive study in the future. Considering he has done this with his own money on his own time, and with donations marginally covering the database's ad-free hosting, the site's contribution is significant.

By his estimate, only 2% to 4% of the world's population has hearing sensitive enough to detect the low-frequency Hum and live in an environment conducive to detecting low-pitched ambient noise. White noise such as a running fan or climate control machinery can easily mask the sound. "Hearers" or "Hummers," as they are sometimes called, generally report the Hum louder during the night than in the day, and even more easily detected indoors than outside. Sadly, those combined features make sleeping difficult, a common complaint.

Dr. MacPherson argues that tinnitus is an unlikely source of the Hum. This condition, caused by damage to the inner ear by external noise, most often produces a constant high-pitched hum, which could not account for most "Hummers." Normal ear physiology could produce otoacoustic emission, or spontaneous noise generated by the inner ear itself. This is a common condition similar to tinnitus in rare cases, but more likely to produce the low-frequency noise associated with the Hum. It would also help explain "Hummers" insisting the noise follows them everywhere, even while traveling long distances.

Causes and Cures for Kokomo Hum

Oddly enough, the Netflix series *Stranger Things* has renewed interest in the Kokomo Hum, since the supernatural soap opera takes place in fictional Hawkins, Indiana. Before the series aired, the public Hum debate ended briefly in 2004, when Kokomo hired an acoustic expert to track down its source. In a short time he pronounced a two culprits: a cooling fan on the Daimler Chrysler's Kokomo Casting Plant and wonky compressors at

Haynes International, both large factories in the city. The companies repaired the troublesome machines and a grateful Kokomo listened and heard...The Hum. Still there. This time, their complaints were generally ignored.

Today, the only effective therapy for "Hummers" has been simply cognitive therapy, with victims learning management skills to stop focusing on the sound. For many, it has worked. But not for everyone.

Mysterious 'Kokomo hum' persists

By Lesley Stedman Weidenbener

Gannett News Service

KOKOMO, Ind. – Despite efforts to silence it, Julie Smith still hears the sound.

Sometimes it reminds her of a tractor-trailer rig idling. Other times, it sounds like distant traffic on an expressway.

It's what has come to be known as the "Kokomo hum" – a mysterious, low-level duced as many questions as answers.

James Cowan, a researcher at Acentech Inc. of Massachusetts, measured low-frequency noise at the homes of several people – including Smith, who complains of headaches and neck aches.

He traced sounds to two factories: DaimlerChrysler's Kokomo Casting Plant and Haynes International, a manufacturer of metal alloys. At both plants, company officials say they have completed work to hush the noise.

But Cowan's study could not determine whether the sounds can be linked to the illnesses experienced by some residents.

Most people can hear sounds between 20 and 20,000 hertz; the lowest key on a piano is about 30 hertz. For most people, tones below 20 hertz can't be heard.

Science, not Pseudoscience

Unlike the research of many Indiana oddities, the Kokomo Hum has both a fair share of crackpot theorists AND reputable researchers. Some of the more laughable theories include weaponized microwave emissions used by the US government, atmospheric electromagnetic radiation produced by the US government, underground nuclear testing by the US government...You get the picture.

Colorful as they are, conspiracy theorists always provide more grammar errors than good evidence. A vast conspiracy involving the US government is very unlikely.

Researchers like Dr. MacPherson have kept the Hum in the realm of reality through hard work, largesse, and real scientific curiosity. Even with his efforts, we may have little chance of uncovering the cause of the Hum, but one thing is certain— without his efforts, there's no chance at all.

Bigfoot in Indiana?

By Tim Bean

Have zoologists uncovered evidence of Bigfoot roaming the rolling hills of southern Indiana or the flat farmland in the north? That depends on whom you talk to.

According to the Bigfoot Field Researchers Organization, seventy-eight reports have been filed from the Hoosier state in the last five decades, all claiming an encounter with Bigfoot.

Considering the beast's locale is traditionally focused on the Pacific Northwest, that's somewhat surprising. Even more surprising is that these seventy-eight sightings have largely gone unreported in the media or scientific community. In fact, the scientific community doesn't even consider Bigfoot research a legitimate branch of primatology, but pseudoscience (like Chinese medicine, chiropractic medicine, alchemy, or astrology).

How can an animal pursued by thousands of researchers and followed by millions of viewers NOT be taken seriously? To uncover that, we have to answer a few shorter questions first.

What is science?

The essence of science is simple. Once upon a time, humans insisted certain ideas were true, then looked for observations supporting those ideas. This was a random crap shoot. Sometimes it worked. Mostly it didn't.

Then a dude named Galileo decided to try something new: he made observations, carefully recorded them, and then created ideas supported by those observations. His most popular discover being a solar system orbiting around the Sun rather than the Earth.

As most know, his peers met his insight with derision and hate. Labeled a heretic, he was placed under house arrest. His new method eventually became science as we know it, a method that has brought us everything from NICU incubators to antibiotics to the very device you are now holding in your hand.

What the h— does this have to do with Bigfoot?

Everything.

Let's take a look at the seventy-eight Indiana sightings of Bigfoot and the evidence these sightings present. The seventy-eight reports the Bigfoot Field Researchers Organization contains are spread over dozens of counties in Indiana, and the reports are divided into Class A, Class B, and Class C. The hefty sounding Class A report details an actual observation of a Bigfoot, and Class B seems to be an indirect sighting of the creature, such as unidentifiable grunting or moaning ("vocalizations" according to the site).

The problem with this evidence (anyone in law enforcement experiences this on a daily basis) is that these observations are all based on self-reporting, meaning it is substantiated only by the person making the report. People sometimes have motives other than the honest truth when making claims. Attention, delusion, greed, ignorance...you name it. Let's look at an example:

In Indiana, Monroe County has the largest number of "observations," but their ambiguity makes them near useless.

November, 1979: Daytime sighting.

May, 1982: Three fishermen watched by "something".

November, 1988: Man recalls his observation of a creature crossing a road....

October, 1989 or 1990: Two sisters observe creature cross the road.

Fall, 2006: Possible encounter while backpacking in the Hoosier National Forest.

March, 2009: Man hears multiple moans and sees a gray creature outside of Bloomington.

<u>October, 2009</u>: Loud, early morning vocalizations heard by duck hunters on Lake Monroe.

Folks, that is NOT how scientists make observations.

So why do networks like the Travel Channel, the History Channel, and the Discovery Channel have entire series dedicated to Bigfoot? Just to waste our time and make money?

You don't think a network would slap together a bunch of half-baked tales and questionable authorities, frame it with some nice graphics and then package it with advertising just to make a quick buck, do you?

Folks, they're simply trying to take advantage of people for profit, and sleep very well on beds made of money.

What about all the scientists that believe Bigfoot exists?

Science is bloodthirsty and brutal. Scientists compete with one another so heavily that a symposium is more like the Thunderdome with manners and lattes. Every minute of every day, scientists look for the errors and weaknesses in the arguments of their peers in order to tear down one conclusion in favor of another. Consequentially, they look for the weaknesses in their own conclusions as a defense against attack. What the average citizen scientist sees as a text-heavy academic journal is actually gladiatorial combat in print. That might sound ridiculous, but just talk to anyone doing original academic research.

It is this viciousness that allows Darwin's Theory of Evolution to remain intact after a century-and-a-half, or Einstein's Theory of General Relativity to hold true even after a century of nit-picking Be aware, *theory* in this sense means "a well-confirmed explanation of nature consistent with the scientific method."

Someone out there is going to chime in with distinctions between theories, Theories, and Laws. Yes, yes, but I want to keep this simple.

When an overwhelming majority of scientists agree on something, that is called having a *consensus*. Scientists have formed a *consensus* on gravity, a spherical (-ish) Earth, bacteria, vaccines, and even climate change (sorry, folks, but yeah). A *consensus* is a big deal because working scientists are like chickens in a coop. If they see weakness or an injury in a peer, they all fall on that weakness in a blue of sharp beaks and squawking, leaving nothing behind but bloodstained feathers. Conspiracy would require large groups working together, and believe me, scientists don't work well together.

The "brave" scientists that take a stand against these theories are generally cheating in their use of the scientific method and avoid real academic scrutiny. If you want to continue the Thunderdome metaphor, imagine a fighter so overmatched he or she digs a hole, escapes the dome and runs away…then lies about how they overpowered their foes. That's not exactly brave.

Does that mean Bigfoot research is useless?

This is a tricky question, because no data is useless, if gathered in the right way, and it certainly doesn't mean the existence of Bigfoot is impossible. It just means it is very, very, very unlikely. If faced with an actual piece of evidence—a body part, a living or dead specimen that's intact, an untouched photo or video that withstands serious scrutiny, any good scientist would be more than willing to accept the possibility. That shouldn't sound overly hopeful. In the centuries of Bigfoot myths, from the Native-American tales to today, not one piece of evidence has ever been placed at the feet of reputable primatologists which held water long.

What about [FILL IN THE BLANK] evidence?

I have seen two pieces of evidence that Bigfoot enthusiasts seem to tout as selling points for their theories.

The first: in 2013, ZooBank, the international organization that catalogs scientific names for living organisms assigned the Latin name *Homo sapiens cognatus* to Bigfoot, thereby labeling Bigfoot as a subspecies of modern humans. Very official sounding. But how about ZooBank's official follow up to this classification?

"ZooBank and the ICZN (International Coalition on Zoological Nomenclature) do not review evidence for the legitimacy of organisms to which names are applied…"

Meaning they just type in the names. It's up to us to decide if the animal is real or not.

The second piece of evidence is the peer-reviewed work of Melba Ketchum, a veterinarian that claimed to possess a human-primate crossbreed. Her work was published in the DeNovo Journal of Science. What might be left out is that only one issue of this journal was ever published, and this single volume contained only one study: Ketchum's. That is known as *bullshit*.

I could go on an on, but I don't need to.

But what if I enjoy searching for Bigfoot?

More power to you. If you enjoy climbing up and down hills and looking for evidence, then that's your right as an American, as long as no one gets hurt. But understand that if you want research to be accepted by the scientific community, then you need to follow the rules of the scientific community, which are stringent, fair and almost five centuries old.

The Indiana City that Once Defined America

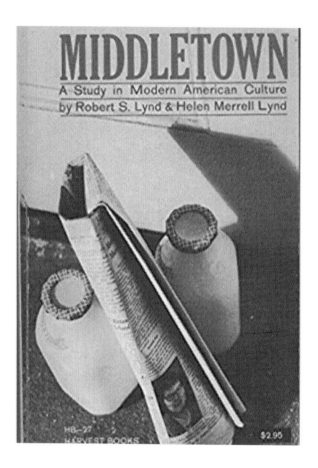

By Mary Giorgio

In 1929, the city of Muncie, Indiana, became famous when it served as the research subject for Robert and Helen Lynd's famous sociological study, *Middletown*. Although the Lynds attempted to keep the city's identity a secret by referring to it simply as Middletown, it didn't take long for Americans to figure out that the city in the study was Muncie, Indiana. The revelation catapulted Muncie into the national spotlight.

Robert and Helen Lynd wondered if American culture had changed significantly as a result of the rapid economic progress of the Second Industrial Revolution. They chose Muncie because it was an average American city. The Lynds extensively researched the city, pouring over old newspapers, city documents, and statistics. They also conducted interviews and surveys of Muncie's white residents. The Lynds ignored African-American culture in the study, claiming it was too small a population.

The resulting book, *Middletown: A Study in Modern American Culture*, received rave reviews. The Lynds categorized their findings into six groups, under which they found that all American activities fell: making a living, keeping house, caring for children, leisure, practicing religion, and community activity. This was true for both working-class and upper-class people.

One of the most important findings in the Middletown study was that the American myth of upward mobility did not ring true. The city was split into two main residential areas - a wealthy enclave and lower class residential section. Which side of town a person was born on determined future opportunities or lack thereof. A staggering 70% of the city's population was working class, but the best career opportunities and political power were almost exclusively reserved for members of the upper class.

The Lynds were also extremely curious about the social effects of major leisure inventions, such as the radio and the automobile. The Lynds found the inventions had redefined the way Americans viewed and experienced leisure time. For example, automobile ownership allowed families to take vacations across America. About 2/3 of Middletown residents owned cars, although the type of car owned depended on economic means.

The study concluded that for the most part, cultural norms did not change in conjunction with rapid economic and industrial development. In the 1930s, the Lynds were approached by their publisher with the idea to write a sequel to their Middletown study. With the economic upheaval of the Great Depression, the second study explored the extent to which this turmoil had impacted social and cultural norms. Published in 1937, the study concluded that while Americans temporarily change their ways during times of economic hardship, as soon as that hardship lifts, they fall back into familiar patterns. The takeaway, then, was that America's cultural norms did not change over time despite periods of rapid development or economic upheaval.

Today, the Middletown studies continue to be regarded as classic sociological investigations into American culture. Sociologists have flocked to Muncie in the ensuing decades to conduct their own research in what has come to be regarded as the quintessential American city. Ball State University established the Center for Middletown Studies in 1980 to continue the city's tradition of sociological scholarship. The original Middletown study may be 90 years old, but remains a legacy for the Muncie community.

Browse Vincennes' Rare Book Collection

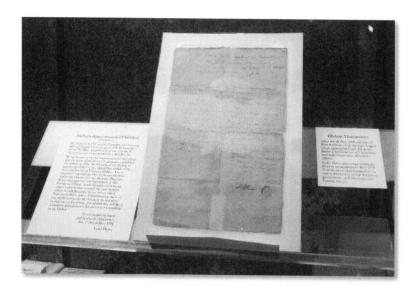

By Mary Giorgio

Nestled behind an old cathedral in Vincennes, Indiana, sits a nondescript building containing valuable treasures. Indiana's oldest library contains rare books and documents dating as far back as 1319. Today, visitors to the Old Cathedral Library & Museum can marvel at the historic artifacts and documents on display.

The idea for a library had its origins in 1794, when Father Benedict Joseph Flagler, pastor of St. Francis Xavier parish in Vincennes, Indiana, established the community's first library. Priests in frontier towns were often the most educated residents, and many took on the mantle of educators. Father Flagler established a small community library used to help teach local residents to read. The library is thought to be the earliest in the state's history.

The library expanded greatly under the watchful eye of the first Bishop of Vincennes, **Simon Gabriel Brute de Remur**. Bishop Brute grew up in France, where his family ran a printing shop. Reverend Brute developed a love for reading and scholarship, graduating first of his class from the School of Medicine in Paris in 1803.

He subsequently joined the priesthood in 1808, embarking on a journey to America. Reverend Brute worked in a number of American universities before being named Bishop of the newly created Diocese of Vincennes in 1834. President John Adams once referred to Bishop Brute as "the most learned a man of his day in America."

Bishop Brute's expansive collection of books was said to have been floated down the Ohio River on a flatboat then delivered to the Vincennes rectory by wagon. By the time he died in 1839, Bishop Brute's collection numbered 8,000 volumes. Subsequent bishops and parish priests maintained the bishop's library. In 1840, Bishop Celestine de la Hailandicre built a library on church grounds to house the remarkable collection.

While the original library still stands, the collection is now housed in a more modern facility. The building includes temperature-controlled vaults for artifact and document storage. The building was funded by a grant from the Eli Lilly Endowment.

The items housed inside the library include books, documents, and artifacts. In all, there are around 12,000 volumes in the collection. The oldest document is a Papal Bull issued by Pope John XXII in 1319. The collection's oldest book is a 13th century manuscript printing of the Book of Psalms, hand printed on sheepskin by a German Benedictine monk. Other treasures include prehistoric tools, 18th and 19th century Bibles, old maps, a peace pipe belonging to Governor William Henry Harrison, Tecumseh's war club, and a 1767 British census document for Vincennes. The town's oldest surviving record, a marriage document dated April 21, 1749, is also housed at the facility.

Located at 205 Church Street, visitors are welcome during summer months and by appointment. The grounds also contain the oldest cathedral in Indiana, dating to 1826, an old rectory built in 1841, and a French and Indian cemetery containing the graves of more than 4,000 of the state's earliest settlers.

Hoosier Cabinets: The Swiss Army Knife of American Cabinetry

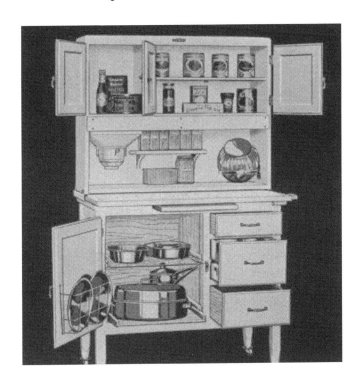

By Mary Giorgio

Today they are coveted antique store or flea market finds, but Hoosier Cabinets were once a kitchen staple in American households. Pre-dating modern homes with built-in kitchen cabinetry, Hoosier Cabinets fulfilled a need for storage and workspace. Many of these early cabinets were designed by the Hoosier Manufacturing Company, from which the term "Hoosier Cabinet" originated.

The first Hoosier Cabinets appeared on the market around 1898. They were designed as a convenience for American households, promising to save women valuable meal prep time. Families could store tools, supplies, and ingredients at arm's reach while using the cabinet's generous counter space to prepare meals.

Freestanding kitchen cabinets began as utilitarian units but soon evolved to include many helpful novelties. There was a place to store flour, sugar, spices, and tools. They were cupboards for appliances. Some units had a meat grinder attachment or cookbook stand. Spice organizers and flour sifters became especially popular. Special glassware was even made to custom fit in the units.

The Hoosier Manufacturing Company quickly rose to fame as sales of their cabinet units took off. The company was one of the earliest manufacturers of Hoosier Cabinets and quickly became the largest manufacturer of the product. It began operations in

Albany, Indiana, in 1898, but later relocated to New Castle. Their great success was likely due to an emphasis on marketing. Ads for their cabinet appeared in popular national magazines like *The Ladies Home Journal* and *The Saturday Evening Post*.

In 1910, the cost of a Hoosier Cabinet ranged from $29 to $49 ($700 to $1,200 today). By 1920, the company had sold two million cabinets. During their peak years in the 1920s, they produced almost 700 cabinets each day. The company even offered a payment plan to help family support their product. For one dollar, a family could take possession of a Hoosier cabinet and keep it as long as they pay a monthly installment of one dollar.

While the Hoosier Manufacturing Company was the largest manufacturer of Hoosier Cabinets in the United States, many smaller Indiana companies successfully produced versions of the cabinet. The second largest-manufacturer was G. I. Sellers Company, which was founded in 1888 in Kokomo, Indiana. The company later relocated to Elwood. By 1922, G. I. Sellers produced 75,000 to 85,000 Hoosier Cabinets per year. Other manufacturers included Boone Kitchen Cabinets based in Lebanon and Coppes Brothers & Zook in Nappanee.

By the late 1920s, new homes began to feature built-in kitchen cabinets. The demand for Hoosier Cabinets declined. By 1935, most Americans consider them to be old-fashioned. The Hoosier Manufacturing Company was sold in 1942 and subsequently liquidated. G. I. Sellers closed in 1950. Other companies, like Coppes Brothers & Zook, embraced the cabinet evolution and transitioned their sales to built-in units. Coppes Brothers & Zook continues its business today.

Today, Hoosier Cabinets are valuable antiques. Restored cabinets can fetch far more than they were originally worth. Some companies even specialize in modern reproductions of the iconic units. For anyone interested in learning more about the cabinetry, the Hoosier Cabinet Museum in Nappanee, Indiana, houses a wide array of historic styles and designs.

From Field to Food: Three Historic Grist Mills

By Mary Giorgio

At one time, they were essential machines all across rural Indiana communities. Indiana's historic grist mills not only processed flour from wheat and cornmeal from corn, but often served as gathering places and social centers in early rural communities. Most have long been demolished, but across Indiana, Hoosiers can still find a few of these historic mills.

One of the oldest grist mills in Indiana, Beck's Mill in Salem, was constructed in 1807. George Beck chose the site at the head of the Blue River when the area was still unsettled. The next year, a fort was built nearby. In 1814, the town of Salem formally incorporated. In the heyday of railroad activity in Indiana, the Monon Railroad purchased cornmeal from Beck's Mill as gifts for its team of rail agents every year.

Beck's Mill

The current mill building dates to 1864 and continued operations until 1950. It was listed on the National Register of Historic Places in 2007. Beck's Mill is the only extant mill in Indiana that exclusively used a grindstone for its entire milling process. Today, the mill has been restored to operational condition and is open on weekends for tours and demonstrations.

Adams Mill

In Cutler, Indiana, John Adams built the area's first mill in 1831. Located along the Wildcat Creek, Adams Mill quickly became a preferred meeting place for the small rural community. At one time, the post office even operated on mill grounds.

The present mill building dates to 1846. After it had closed in 1951, the mill became a popular local attraction featuring demonstrations of early grain grinding practices. The mill was listed on the National Register of Historic Places in 1984 and today houses a museum of rural America.

Woods Mill

In Hobart, Indiana, the Woods Historic Grist Mill dates to 1876. It is widely thought to be the first industrial site in Lake County. In 1838, John Woods built a sawmill on the site. In 1839, he built his first grist mill on the banks of Deep River. Both did a brisk business from nearby settlers and farmers.

The present mill is powered by a tube wheel rather than the more common water wheel. Today, the mill sits within Deep River Country Park. The mill is still operational and offers demonstrations of the process of grinding cornmeal from May to October. It was listed on the National Register of Historic Places in 1976.

With historic mills once operating in almost every corner of the Hoosier state, thousands of visitors can experience a bit of pioneer history at these fascinating sites each year.

"If It Flies, It Dies": Exploring Indiana's C-47 Nike Missile Site

By Tim Bean

Staring at a stretch of concrete littered with forty years of trespassing, vandalism, and weeds, it's easy to view the entire Nike Missile Program as millions of wasted dollars.

Twenty years, 265 sites, 40 strategic defense areas, round-the-clock staffing, updates, training, technology, construction, and eventual decommissioning—all of this carrying a price tag so staggering, estimating it in 2019 dollars would turn your stomach.

History in hindsight is always deceptively simple: Rome traded democracy for dictatorship. Feudalism ended with the longbow. Literacy began with the Plague. Never fight a Russian winter.

There is no simplifying history; only oversimplifying it.

In reality, think of the Nike Missile Program and the C-47 Site like this:

Imagine jumping out of a plane with not one parachute, but ten carefully-packed parachutes. As you plummet to the ground, you pull the rip cords, only to find each parachute has failed, one by one. When you got to that tenth and final chute, wouldn't you regard it with reverence? Wouldn't it become something more than thread, silk, and wire? —*Please, please work, PLEASE*—

THAT was the Nike Missile Program.

If nuclear war had ever arrived, and the Soviet bombers and/or ICBMs eluded Strategic Air Command's first-strike, NATO defenses, waves of American fighters AND anti-aircraft missiles, then these scattered Nike missile bases were the last line of defense for 40 regions across the United States, including Chicago and Northwest Indiana. Those sites stood against an unimaginable tapestry of horror, suffering, and death that is nuclear war.

Thinking of it like that, adjusting for inflation seems a little ridiculous.

Project Nike: 1953-1973

From 1953 to 1973, approximately 265 Nike Missile Sites protected 40 defense areas across the United States. The rudimentary delivery systems for nuclear weapons in the early 1950s necessitated a focus on cities and concentrated industrial or strategic targets. The "overkill" strategy of mutually-assured destruction would not arrive for another decade or so.

The purpose of Project Nike was entirely defensive; an effort to fortify the likeliest targets in the United States and eliminate the chance of Soviet success in nuclear attack. These sites, which formed asymmetrical clusters called "Defense Areas," served the same function as anti-aircraft gun batteries had during World War II.

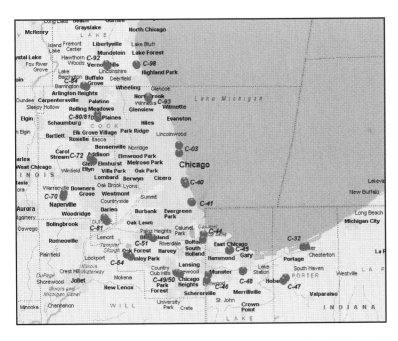

EACH BLUE DOT IS A FORMER NIKE SITE IN THE CHICAGO/GARY AREA

Jet propulsion and high altitude bombardment had rendered AA guns obsolete. Project Nike merged the budding 1950's technology of computers, radar systems, and rocket propulsion in a single package. The result was a weapon that exceeded Mach 2, had an effective range of 25 miles, and utilized advanced radar guidance data to adapt to changes in target altitude, direction, and speed.

Development and testing took several years, since the engineers of Project Nike were creating the world's first surface-to-air missile. Once the Nike Ajax had proved itself again and again in live fire demonstrations, the US Army quickly began replacing the nearly one thousand AA batteries across the US with Nike launch sites. By the early 60s, 265 Nike bases dotted the US.

Each Nike missile site differed in layout, depending on local topography, but all shared three major components: a launcher area, a control or administrative area, and at least three radar towers.

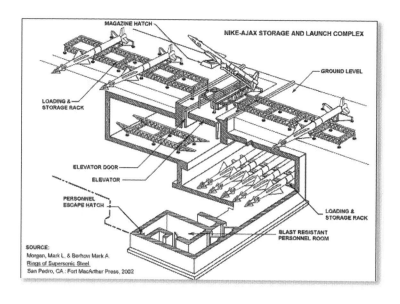

Military policy required a half-mile separation between the control and launcher areas, so control staff would be protected in case of an accidental missile explosion. Multiple radar towers allowed Nike computers to acquire, track, and guide multiple missiles simultaneously. Combined with a rigorously-trained staff and efficient launcher design, a single Nike battery could fire nearly a missile a minute at approaching targets.

In the case of Northwest Indiana's C-47 base (which contained three launch batteries), that meant a fire rate of one Ajax every twenty seconds. Add that to the 19 other Nike sites in the Chicago-Gary Defense Area, you have a blanket of supersonic destruction with which Soviet bombers had to contend. A good fight.

Going Nuclear: Nike-Hercules

Despite its reliability and accuracy, the Nike Ajax had a significant flaw; when approaching grouped target formations, its control and radar systems tended to see clustered targets (such as a wing of Soviet bombers) as a single target, resulting in the Ajax's premature detonation with no damage to target aircraft.

Additionally, the Soviet military's addition of ICBMs (Intercontinental Ballistic Missiles) to its nuclear arsenal posed a challenge for the Ajax, which had an operational flight ceiling of 70,000 feet and a top speed of Mach 2.25. While effective against a long-range bomber, those performance specs do little against an ICBM reentry vehicle traveling at speeds exceeding Mach 5. While designers originally intended to simply mount a small nuclear warhead on the Ajax, they ultimately decided an improved surface-to-air missile utilizing the same launch platform as the Ajax would be a better investment.

NIKE AJAX ON FAR RIGHT; NIKE HERCULES ON FAR LEFT

This redesign, first called the Nike B, then the Nike-Hercules, was a significant upgrade from the Ajax. The Hercules used only solid fuel as a propellent, rather than liquid fuel, improving the missile's safety and rate of fire. It also posed a significant threat for bombers and ICBMs. With an effective range of almost 100 miles, a flight ceiling of 100,000 feet, and a top speed of Mach 3.65, it functioned well as an area denial defensive weapon. To provide these performance boosts in short order, military engineers simply bolted four Nike-Ajax boosters together to create a single Hercules' booster.

The most significant change was the replacement of a conventional warhead with a nuclear one, allowing a single missile to destroy multiple targets and increase its chances of success against an ICBM. The Hobart C-47 Nike missile site was among the first to receive the nuclear-armed Hercules (a 20-kiloton warhead, roughly the yield as the Nagasaki bomb).

Ending an Era

For twenty years, the Nike sites provided 24-hour protection against an impending Soviet attack, but by the mid-1960s, the number of ICBMs in the Soviet and American arsenals rendered the defensive capability of the Nike sites obsolete. In 1965, Soviet and American military each possessed around 30,000 nuclear warheads in a variety of forms, with enough potential to destroy human civilization twenty times over.

Things had, uh, gotten out of hand.

In 1972, the United States sacrificed the aging Nike program as a concession in the SALT I talks (Strategic Arms Limitation Treaty) and by 1974, almost all Nike sites were decommissioned*, including all those in the Chicago-Gary Defense Area. Missiles and equipment were dismantled, repurposed, or scrapped, leaving behind only the immovable structures.

In the 1970s, my father was among the military personnel to decommission and scrap site C-45 near the Gary Municipal Airport.

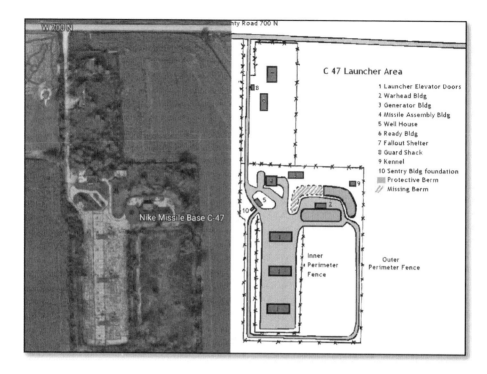

C 47 Launcher Area

1 Launcher Elevator Doors
2 Warhead Bldg
3 Generator Bldg
4 Missile Assembly Bldg
5 Well House
6 Ready Bldg
7 Fallout Shelter
8 Guard Shack
9 Kennel
10 Sentry Bldg foundation
▓ Protective Berm
// Missing Berm

Nike Missile Base C-47

Inner
Perimeter
Fence

Outer
Perimeter Fence

C-47 LAUNCHER AREA: GPS IMAGE & MAP

Contrary to rumors, the C-47 site is NOT an abandoned parcel of land, but a National Historic Site and therefore, protected. I toured the facility myself recently, under the unofficial purveyance of amateur historian and county park employee. To be more specific, I know what I shouldn't touch.

In Northwest Indiana, the site is no great secret, as evidenced by the tapestry of graffiti covering the structure. Across the entire launch site, the only item in good repair was the swinging gate guarding its entrance. Everything else had been tragically left to the elements. YouTube videos and image searches prove the site has been crawled over again and again, yet I have seen nothing hinting at its historic importance.

C-47 ENTRANCE GATE (NOTICE THE FRESH PAINT)

C-47 is the only complete base remaining out of the 19 in the Chicago-Gary Defense Area. The Control or Administration Area is now leased to a paintball facility known as Blast Camp, which creatively wove the site's history into its company branding. The original buildings (including the radar towers) remain relatively intact in both areas. Coupled with that is the site's early use of the nuclear-armed Nike-Hercules.

REMAINS OF THE GUARD SHACK

MISSILE ASSEMBLY BUILDING

ELEVATOR DOORS AND ENTRANCE, WITH ESCAPE
HATCH PARTIALLY VISIBLE ON LEFT.

The C-47 site was designated "historic" in 1998, yet nothing has been done since then, other than installing a new lock on the site's swinging gate. Odds are are no local, county, state, or federal officials will do anything significant with the site. Instead, like too many historic structures, C-47 will suffer the humiliation of slow decay and cryptic graffiti. *That is a damn tragedy.*

My hope is that a company or private donor might take an interest in the site and restore it, so guided tours might be possible. A water pump and generator, a half-dozen weed whackers, herbicide, some scrub brushes, and a small army of volunteers could transform the site in a few months.

My own visit was brief; the forest of weeds surrounding the buildings made entry too difficult, and the temperature hovered near 100. I snapped my pictures and vowed to return when cold weather has thinned the greenery, making exploration easier.

LAUNCHER ACCESS DOOR, FLOODED UNDERGROUND

The shock of seeing the crumbling, vandalized buildings being swallowed by weeds didn't anger as much as sadden me. Those of who have lived in and near Chicago and Northwest Indiana, or have family from this area, owe a debt to the site and to the soldiers that staffed it. Few things are more political or controversial than nuclear weapons, but this site's purpose was only defensive. Not only defensive, but our LAST DEFENSE.

Through two decades of both the imagined and actual horrors of the Cold War, soldiers manned this (and all) Nike sites 24-hours a day, ready in a moment to protect citizens from nuclear annihilation. To me, the current fate of C-47 is far less than it deserves. A long-term preservation is preferable to a quick razing, but anything is better than the slow decay.

Nike Missile Bases in the Movies

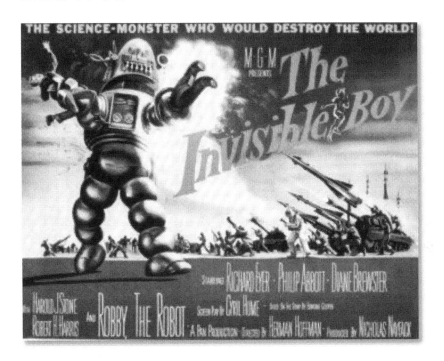

THE SCIENCE-MONSTER WHO WOULD DESTROY THE WORLD!

M-G-M PRESENTS The Invisible Boy

STARRING RICHARD EYER · PHILIP ABBOTT · DIANE BREWSTER

HAROLD J. STONE · ROBERT H. HARRIS AND ROBBY THE ROBOT · Screen Play by CYRIL HUME · A Pan Production · Directed by HERMAN HOFFMAN · Produced by NICHOLAS NAYFACK

Before diving into the Hollywood repurposing of these Cold War artifacts, let me clear something up: my fascination for the past, present, and future of Project Nike isn't born from cynicism or a morbid fascination with a full-scale nuclear exchange (I once read through a one-inch stack of accounts by Hiroshima victims and wish that I had not).

These Nike missile batteries (*batteries*, not *silos*, which are vertical structures used to store and launch medium and long-range ballistic missiles) spent two decades guarding the front door of dozens of American cities and millions of lives. They were entirely defensive in nature. The radar, missile, and tracking technology utilized at these bases became a kind of "gold standard" in missile defense systems even today.

We never had to find out if they would have worked against bombers or a salvo of Soviet ICBMs. Had that day actually come, I think those Nike batteries and the soldiers manning them could have put up one hell of a good fight.

As well-designed and well-maintained as they were, most of the nearly 300 Nike bases have disappeared. Some bases and buildings have been reused and redesigned, but most were razed to make way for American life. Nothing wrong with that, although I wish a few more (Hobart's C-47 included) would see some TLC in the interest of historic preservation.

A scant handful, however, were immortalized not in history books or museums, but on the big screen. These Nike bases have been used as backdrops or sets in Hollywood movies, although none were exactly Academy Award contenders. Readers may have seen one or two of these obscure films, and this article may inspire you seek them out. Don't blame me if the movie stinks. I'm only here for the history.

The Invisible Boy (1957)

Robbie (sometimes spelled Robby) the Robot became the breakout star of 1956's *The Forbidden Planet*, but MGM decided that the heavy cost involved in creating Robbie necessitated his starring in another movie. Thus was born the confusing and forgettable science-fiction film *The Invisible Boy*, released the same year the Soviets launched Sputnik.

NOTICE THE LAUNCH ELEVATOR, CENTER-RIGHT

The plot is...terrible and I don't want to summarize it, but during the film's climax, as Robbie is wading through American military forces to reach his rocket, you can clearly see the line of deployed Nike-Ajax missiles in the foreground. Shooting took place at LA-55, one of the 19 bases surrounding Los Angeles, with the permission of the military, who were much friendlier to film makers during the days of the Hays Code. Bad movie, but it's fascinating to see a Nike base in its freshly-painted prime.

Escape from the Planet of the Apes (1971)

The original *Planet of the Apes* franchise went heavy on social consciousness, and critics revere *Escape from the Planet of the Apes*, the third of five films, as one of the franchise's best. In the film, three ape characters are sent back in time to 1973 America, where they are imprisoned and studied by the American military. Although much of the movie is filmed on routine Hollywood sound stages, several key scenes were filmed at the LA-78 Nike Nike missile base, specifically the control and administration areas.

Studio executives loved the idea of the apes arriving in modern America, mostly because it was very cost-effective. The film starred Hollywood heavies Roddy McDowell, Kim Hunter, and Sal Mineo in his final film role.

ESTABLISHING SHOT FROM *ESCAPE* FILM

Wavelength (1983)

Two weeks ago they landed on Earth. Today, beneath a major American city, the experiments begin...

The Alien Terror is here on Earth!

WAVELENGTH

Wavelength recycled the E.T. formula (misunderstood alien/big, bad government/wide-eyed young man between) shamelessly. Starring David Carradine and Cherie Currie (of The Runaways), Wavelength's artwork and soundtrack by Tangerine Dream are generally considered its best elements. Plot? The military has stored and experimented on a group of bald, expressionless aliens whose childlike appearance is meant to tug at our hearts, but instead gives a pretty hefty *Village of the Damned* vibe.

This film differs in that the abandoned Nike base becomes an active plot element—why does an abandoned base need THAT much power?—but it is unclear if it was actually filmed at a Nike base.

SPOOKY SHOT OF ABANDONED NIKE BASE IN FILM

My guess is yes. Since so many were still standing and in relatively good shape in the early 80s, there's no reason not to use one in the filming.

The film is also infamous in that a few former military personnel claim it's a true story. Of course they have no evidence, but when has that stopped anyone from proselytizing?

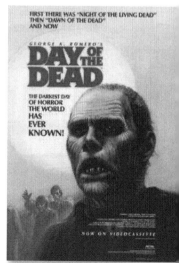

Dawn of the Dead (1985)

Probably the most famous movie on this

list, 1985's *Day of the Dead* holds personal relevance for me because of a video rental mixup. When I was six, my father rented a kids' film for us, popped it in the VCR, and walked out to do the dishes. He returned 15 minutes later to three silent and wide-eyed children.

The store clerk had accidentally switched the films, and three kids (8, 6, and 5) were psychologically imprinted with 15 minutes of zombies lumbering down a dusty street, a headless corpse kicking its legs, a misbehaving zombie brought down with a drill bit to the forehead...And a long launch elevator yawning open to provide shelter for the movie's heroes.

NOT A NIKE ELEVATOR

Three elements made up the abandoned Nike base. The topside shot was constructed for the film itself. Romero used a limestone mine as a stand in for the cavernous shelter, but the scene where the heroes ride the elevator platform down to safety is an actual Nike base outside Pittsburgh.

ACTUAL NIKE ELEVATOR

Finding the references for this handful of movies wasn't easy. Because of the plentiful number of abandoned bases, and the frequent shifts in ownership, there is no doubt many other bases were used as film locations without acknowledgement. The good news is the American military built their Nike missile defense bases to last; the few bases that remain, as long as they receive even cursory maintenance, should be around for many, many years to come.

The South Bend Mansion Built by a Plow

By Mary Giorgio

Listed on the National Register of Historic Places, the Oliver Mansion in South Bend, Indiana, boasts a whopping 38 rooms and over 12,000 square feet. Built in 1897 for industrialist Joseph D. Oliver, the home is a popular destination for tourists passing through the city.

Joseph D. Oliver (a.k.a. JD) was the president of Oliver Chilled Plow Company, a factory founded by his father, James Oliver.

James Oliver was the inventor of the chilled plow, which consisted of a cast iron blade that was stronger and smoother due to a cooling process. He patented the design in 1857.

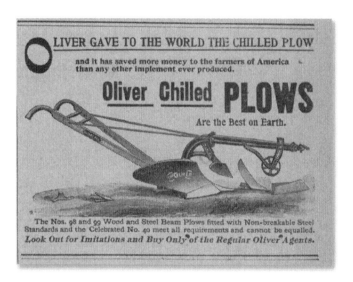

JD began to work for his father in 1867 at the age of 16. He first worked as a bookkeeper, but within a year had been promoted to the role of treasurer. JD would go on to become the company's president. Under his leadership, Oliver Chilled Plow became the biggest plow factory in the world.

In 1885, JD married Anna Wells. The couple had four children. In 1897, JD commissioned an opulent mansion for his family, meant to display their vast wealth. The Romanesque Queen Anne structure was built by New York architect Charles Alonzo Rich. The home was one of the first in South Bend to have electricity. It also boasted an early central vacuum system and burglar alarm.

The family named their new home "Copshaholm," after the Scottish village that James Oliver had immigrated from. Upon completion, JD purchased a large parcel of land adjacent to the mansion. Landscape architect Alice E. Neale of New York City was hired to turn 2.5 acres into an Italian-style garden, complete with rose garden, tea house, and tennis lawn. The family entertained extensively and used the outdoor space for many gatherings.

The mansion stayed in the Oliver family for 72 years. Following the deaths of JD (1933) and Anna (1937), their unmarried daughter Susan Catherine took on the mantle of head of household. She lived in the home until her death in 1970. Her brother, Joseph Jr., also lived in the home until he died in 1972. At that time, JD and Anna's grandchildren donated to the imposing mansion to the Northern Indiana Historical Society.

Today, the home is operated by the South Bend Center for History. The home is set up as it looked in the 1930s, complete with numerous original furnishings. Visitors can see what life would have been like for the family during those years. The home contains numerous works of art, including two bronze busts that were sculpted by famed Chicago artist Lorado Taft. One depicts JD, while the other bust portrays his father James.

The Oliver Mansion is a prominent reminder of South Bend's industrial past. Tours are offered year-round. The home sits on the campus of the Studebaker National Museum and can be accessed through the museum's main entrance gates.

Indiana Invention: Stove Top Stuffing

By Mary Giorgio

In post-World War II years, Americans became obsessed with convenience foods. Prepackaged and easy to assemble cake mixes, pre-sliced bread, TV dinners, instant coffee, and more became popular purchases at the grocery store. In 1971, Indiana native Ruth Siems invented a new addition to the ever-growing list of convenience products available on store shelves: Stove Top Stuffing.

Ruth was born in Evansville, Indiana, in 1931. After graduating from Bosse High School, Ruth enrolled at Purdue University.

There, she earned a bachelor's degree in home economics, graduating in 1953.

After graduating, Ruth returned to Evansville, where she got a job at the General Foods plant. Ruth was assigned to test the quality of cake and flour mixes. After a few years, Ruth relocated to the company's Tarrytown, New York, facility, where she began to work in research and development.

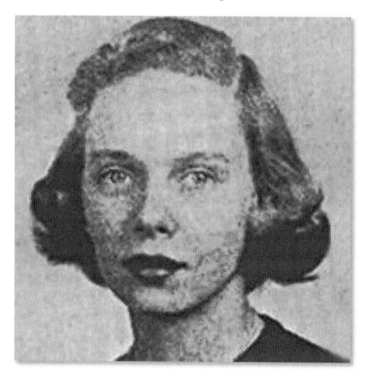

RUTH SIEMS

It was while employed in the research and development department that Ruth became the lead inventor on a project to develop and improve ready-made stuffing mix. Stove Top Stuffing was born. The secret to the recipe's success was the perfect sized breadcrumb, a development the company later patented in 1975.

Delicious, perfectly made stuffing, was now just five minutes away with the addition of water and a little heat.

The product hit shelves in 1971. The company had a great product, but part of the secret to its success lay in General Foods' marketing strategy. Stuffing was ubiquitous with Thanksgiving, but in order to be profitable, the company needed strong year-round sales. Using the tagline, "Stuffing Instead of Potatoes?" General Foods embarked on an ingenious marketing plan to convince Americans that Stove Top Stuffing could replace the starch in their weeknight dinners. The plan was highly successful, and soon Stove Top had become a food icon. Although the side dish is still heavily associated with Thanksgiving meals, today it has become a year-round staple for many families.

The Stove Top brand was purchased by Kraft Foods in 1995. Today, it is available in five flavors: turkey, chicken, beef, cornbread, and sourdough. An estimated 60 million boxes are sold each year.

Ruth worked at General Foods for over 30 years before retiring in 1985. After retiring, she returned home to Indiana. Ruth purchased a historic home in Newburgh, Indiana. She spent her retirement years collecting antiques and restoring historic spinning wheels and looms. She was widely known in her community for her love of sewing. Ruth died on November 13, 2005, and is buried in her hometown of Evansville, Indiana.

Stove Top Stuffing has been in high demand since it first hit product shelves in 1971. Debuting at a time in America when convenience foods were in high demand, Stove Top Stuffing reinvented the way Americans thought about the traditional holiday food. Today, millions of Americans enjoy stuffing year-round.

Unsolved: Indy's 1978 Burger Chef Murders

By Mary Giorgio

Editor's Note: This is not the typical story we run, but being a parent, it's a story I would want told and told until it was solved.

Friday, November 17, 1978. 11 PM.

Four teenage workers were closing up the Speedway Burger Chef restaurant. They were never seen alive again.

The Speedway Burger Chef was part of a large fast-food chain headquartered in Indianapolis. It had numerous locations across town and over 600 nationwide. The chain was bought by Hardee's in the 1980s.

Restaurant employees Jane Friedt, Ruth Shelton, Daniel Davis, and Mark Flemmonds locked up the restaurant at 11 PM. The four teens were scheduled to stay late and clean up before leaving.

Shortly before midnight, a friend stopped by to visit and found the place empty, with the back door ajar.

The teen called the police, who responded to the scene. The safe was open, with over $500 missing. The cash registers were full, and the employees' personal effects were still in the restaurant. Police wrapped up their investigation, assuming it was no more than petty theft by the four employees, and allowed Burger Chef management to clean up and reopen the next day.

But the four weren't seen again. Families, friends, and then police joined in the search. When four bodies were found in rural Johnson County, police realized they had a grisly murder on their hands.

POLICE SEARCH JOHNSON CO. WOODS

Few details of what happened between the hours of 11 PM and midnight are known. Investigators surmised that the robbers must have hidden near the rear exit, waiting for someone to take out the trash. From there, they must have forced their way into the building. A witness later remembered seeing a suspicious car with two men parked outside the Burger Chef near the time of the robbery.

Young Speedway Murder Victims

Miss Friedt Flemmonds Miss Shelton Davis

One theory floated by investigators was that one of the victims must have recognized an attacker, prompting the horrific crime. Regardless of the reason, the four victims were taken from the restaurant alive and driven out to a wooded area in Johnson County. There, they were brutally killed.

Police chased down numerous leads, but were never able to make an arrest. A gang of four robbers who had been active in Indianapolis that fall became prime suspects. Several other Burger Chef locations had been hit. Some members of that crew were later convicted of other robberies, but police were never able to find forensic evidence linking them to the murders.

Additional frustration stemmed from the fact that the murder weapons were never found. Police searched in vain for a knife handle, gun, and chain thought to be used to commit the killings. Lack of progress on the case eventually led investigators to offer a $25,000 reward for an anonymous tip leading to an arrest. Still, no one talked.

Today, it has been more than 40 years since the Burger Chef murders took place, and the crime remains unsolved. Such is the fascination with the case that in 2018, a film crew from Australia visited Indianapolis to search for clues. The crimes may never be solved, but those involved in the investigation still hope to one day bring closure to victims' families.

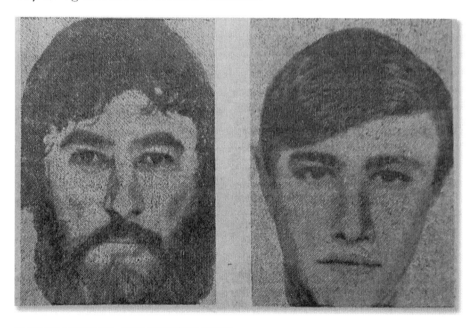

RENDERING OF SUSPECTS

Oops: Hexavalent Chromium Taints Lake Michigan

By Tim Bean

Hexavalent Chromium sounds nasty because it IS nasty.

Chances are you've been exposed to it in a small degree. Stainless steel and chrome. Treated lumber. Fabric dyes. Thousands of products, made here and overseas, contain it. Hoosiers near any manufacturing plant or waterway (which means nearly every Hoosier) have been exposed to it, and most drinking water siphoned from Lake Michigan contains trace amounts.

A recognized carcinogen, hexavalent chromium became the invisible antagonist in 2000's *Erin Brockovich*. Despite its notoriety, the EPA has yet to establish a maximum contaminant level (MCL), leaving control and monitoring to under-funded state or municipal agencies.

These feeble restrictions allowed US Steel to spill hexavalent chromium into Lake Michigan twice in 2018 with little more than bureaucratic slaps on the wrist. The first occurred in April, when fishermen alerted authorities to an over 300-pound spill. US Steel apologized, monitored then dismissed concern and beach closures as "absurd."

Last month another, smaller spill occurred. In fact, US Steel officials didn't feel it was necessary to alert the Indiana Department of Environmental Management (IDEM) to the second spill right away. When they did, they requested it be kept "confidential." The IDEM did just that. News of the spill only came to light after being unearthed by an inquisitive University of Chicago law student. Since this discovery, US Steel has pledged to correct its error by tweaking equipment and retraining employees.

Right now, that's where the story stands. No doubt it will be buried and forgotten until the next spill comes along.

This isn't an editorial about the evils of industry. That's been done ad nauseam. This is an editorial about blame. This entire story, laid out succinctly here, was, in actuality, tangled as though woven by a blind spider. It made finding a target for accusations difficult.

Should US Steel workers be blamed for shoddy work? US Steel itself for poor equipment, training or plain old apathy? US Steel officials for requesting confidentiality? The IDEM for granting that same confidentiality? The EPA for not establishing an MCL? Hoosiers for overreacting? Municipalities for under-reacting? The list goes on and on. Who's to blame? That's up to you.

Whomever you decide, here are the people to contact:

~US Steel Public Relations: 1-219-888-2000

~EPA Regulatory Department: 1-877-378-5457

~Indiana Department of Environmental Management: 1-800-451-6027

~EPA's Great Lake National Program (Lake Michigan): 1-312-886-3451

Gary Own's Lee Calhoun

By Mary Giorgio

Raised in Gary, Indiana, Lee Calhoun became the pride of the
city when he won Olympic gold in the 110-m hurdles in 1956.
Calhoun went on to break a world record and earn a second gold
medal before retiring from the sport in 1960. Long before he was
an Olympic star, however, Calhoun was just an average Hoosier
boy.

Calhoun was born on February 23, 1933, in Laurel, Mississippi.
When he was a toddler, Calhoun moved with his mother and
stepfather to Gary. His stepfather, Rev. Cory Calhoun, served as

pastor of the Evening Star Baptist Church. Eventually, the couple had fourteen children together.

Calhoun attended Roosevelt High School. A talented athlete, he was awarded a scholarship to North Carolina Central University in 1951. There, he was coached by Dr. Levy Walker, who later served as president of the U.S. Olympic committee. Calhoun attended college for two years, but left in 1953 to join the U.S. Army. He returned to the school two years later with a focused ambition to become a star athlete.

TRACK TEAM
Kneeling: Edward Carter, James Watson. . . . *Standing:* William Echols, Leonard Barnett, Bernard Williams, Ernest Simmons.

In 1956, Calhoun won the National Collegiate Athletic Association (NCAA) 120-yard hurdles championship. He also won the Amateur Athletic Association (AAU) 110-m hurdles championship that year. On the heels of these victories, Calhoun competed in the 1956 Olympic Games in Melbourne. Competing in the 110-m hurdles, Calhoun beat his personal best by a full second to win gold. Such was the excitement in Gary, Indiana, that Calhoun returned to a huge parade in his honor.

Calhoun earned his bachelor's degree in 1957 but continued to compete in amateur track and field competitions. He achieved additional NCAA and AAU Championship titles in 1957 and 1959.

Calhoun's career as an amateur athlete hit a roadblock in 1957 after he appeared on the game show, *Bride and Groom*. During the show, Calhoun and his fiancé were married by Calhoun's stepfather. Although producers were unaware that Calhoun was an Olympic star, the AAU accused him of financially benefitting from his status and suspended him from competition. The AAU lifted the ban in 1959, just in time for the lead-up to the 1960 summer Olympics.

On August 21, 1960, Calhoun tied the world record in the 110-m hurdles in Bern, Switzerland. Thereafter, he was favored to win an Olympic gold medal. At the Rome Olympics one month later, Calhoun won gold. He became the first athlete to win gold in that event at two consecutive Olympic games.

Following his second Olympic victory, Calhoun retired from competition. After completing a master's degree, he accepted a position as track coach at Grambling State University (1967-70). He later coached track at Yale (1971-80) and Western Illinois University (1980-89). During those years, Calhoun twice served as an assistant Olympic coach. He was respected for his integrity and tireless commitment to his athletes.

Calhoun died in 1989 at the age of 56. Following his death, the Lee Calhoun Memorial Invitational was established at Western Illinois University. Calhoun is remembered as one of several famed athletes to have graduated from Gary's Roosevelt High School, often mentioned alongside Charles Adkins, (Olympic boxer), Dick Barnett (pro-basketball star), Lloyd McClendon (pro-baseball player), and Willie Williams (Olympic track star).

Songwriter Cole Porter: from Indiana to Broadway

By Mary Giorgio

Mention the name "Cole Porter" and most Americans will conjure the image of a great Broadway talent. During his career, Porter wrote well over 100 Broadway songs. He was also one of the few songwriters in his day to provide both lyrics and music. Porter's hits include "Night and Day," "I've Got You Under My Skin," and "Anything Goes." Many people don't know that this famed American composer was a native Hoosier, born and raised in Peru, Indiana.

Porter was born in 1891 in Peru, Indiana. His father was a druggist and his mother was the daughter of James Omar Cole, known at the time as "the richest man in Indiana." Cole had earned his fortune in the coal and timber industries. He was heavily involved in the family's affairs and paid for much of young Porter's education.

PORTER'S PERU BIRTHPLACE

Porter's mother encouraged his interest in music. By age 6, he was taking violin and piano lessons, although he quickly developed a preference for the piano. At age 10, Porter wrote his first operetta, which his mother succeeded in getting published.

At the age of 13, Porter left Indiana to study at Worcester Academy in Massachusetts. He was said to have arrived at the boarding school with his upright piano in tow and made friends by delighting the other boys with his tunes. In 1909, Porter enrolled at Yale University. There, he studied English, music, and French. At Yale, Porter joined many musical groups. He was an early member of the Whittenpoofs *a cappella* group and as a senior, served as president of the Yale Glee Club. During his Yale years, Porter wrote 300 songs, including Yale's famous football fight songs "Bulldog" and "Bingo Eli Yale."

Porter's grandfather insisted that he study law, so in 1913, he enrolled at Harvard Law School. He soon realized that the program was not for him and switched to the music. Porter's mother supported the move, but was said to have hidden the switch from her father.

On the heels of his college career, in 1915, Porter published his first Broadway song, "Esmeralda." It would be more than 10 years, however, before he succeeded in joining the upper echelon of Broadway songwriters. His 1916 Broadway production, *See America First*, was a huge flop.

In 1917, Porter moved to Europe to work with the Duryea Relief Organization during World War I. He later claimed to have joined the French Foreign Legion, but that fact remains subject to debate. Characteristically, Porter brought a portable piano with him on his travels and entertained countless troops with his music.

In 1919, Porter composed his first big hit, "Old Fashioned Garden," for the revue *Hitchy-Koo*. In 1923, his short ballet, *Within The Quota*, was also well-received. The ballet featured one of the earliest symphonic jazz-based compositions. A few years later, in 1928, Porter's musical, *Paris*, became an overnight sensation. The production featured one of his most famous tunes, "Let's Do It." Finally Porter had achieved his dream - acceptance as one of Broadway's top composers.

Throughout the 1930s, Porter continued to compose tunes for hit Broadway musicals. He even dabbled in musical scores for

 movies. Then, in 1937, a serious horseback riding accident left Porter partially paralyzed. In 1948, Porter made a monumental comeback with the success of his musical, Kiss Me, Kate. The musical was performed over 1,000 times in New York and 400 times in London. The show received a Tony for best musical.

Porter was awarded best composer and lyricist. It was the pinnacle of his career, and his last great Broadway hit.

Porter died in 1964, in Santa Monica, California. He continues to be revered as one of Broadway's most talented composers. In 1991, the United States Postal Service issued a stamp in honor of the centennial of his birth. His childhood home in Peru, Indiana, is now a small inn.

E.W. Kelley: Indiana's Food Industry Emperor

By Mary Giorgio

Most of us have eaten at a Steak 'n Shake at some point in our lives. Not many of us know that the brand was revived from the brink of extinction by Indiana-native Estel Wood (E.W.) Kelley. During his career in industry, Kelley established some of America's most iconic food products. As a philanthropist, he gave millions of dollars to higher education development at Indiana University.

Kelley was born in Sharpsville, Indiana, in 1917. His parents were farmers. Kelley grew up learning the value of hard work and received his education from the community's one-room schoolhouse. After high school, Kelley enrolled at Indiana

136

ICE CREAM KLONDIKES

The Biggest Bargain in Town!

6 for 1.49

28¢ EACH...

America's favorite ice cream bar... rich vanilla ice cream with a thick, tasty coating of chocolate. Choose plain or krispy.

University's School of Business. There, he quickly became a student leader. He founded the school's accounting club and served as president of the student body. He graduated in 1939.

Throughout his business career, Kelley worked to develop many popular American products. While running the Bird's Eye division of General Foods, he is credited with suggesting a mix of peas and pearl onions. The mix continues to be a popular product today.

At Fairmount Foods, Kelley helped develop Klondike bars. He also played a leading role in the marketing of Tang and Cool Whip. During his career, Kelley also made significant contributions to the successful introduction of Grey Poupon, A1 Steak Sauce, and Smirnoff vodka.

In 1981, Kelley's Indianapolis-based investment group, E. W. Kelley and Associates, bought the Steak 'n Shake restaurant chain. Steak 'n Shake was originally founded in 1934 by Gus Belt of Normal, Illinois. His diner's burgers and shakes were so beloved that Belt began a small franchise. After his death, the restaurant changed hands several times, struggling to maintain its identity and loyal patron base.

137

Under Kelley's leadership, Steak 'n Shake was revived. Soon, the restaurant had gone from a small, struggling chain to a huge franchise with over 450 locations. The key to Kelley's success was taking the chain back to its roots: quality burgers and shakes served in 1950s-style diners. Some of Kelley's key changes included an updated menu, food made to order and delivered by a server, and use of real China and flatware.

Kelley credited his business success to his education at Indiana University. He remembered his years as a student fondly and ultimately decided to donate millions of dollars to the school. His first gifts were made to Indiana University Kokomo, located near his Sharpsville home.

His donations funded its Kelley Student Center, Kelley House, the library, and a scholarship fund. In 1997, he donated $23 million to establish the Kelley Scholars program at Indiana University's business school. In 1999, Kelley endowed a chair in business administration. Because of his generous contributions, the business school changed its name to the Indiana University Kelley School of Business.

A Hoosier at heart, Kelly maintained a residence in Sharpsville. In 1985, he started a nonprofit organization on his family farm. Over time, the organization restored many of the farm's original buildings for museum use. It continues today as the Kelly Agricultural Historical Museum. The museum serves as an event venue for Tipton County.

Sadly, Kelley passed away in 2003 at 86. A successful businessman and philanthropist, E. W. Kelley's legacy includes the introduction of many iconic brands and a namesake business school at Indiana University. The next time you bite into a famed Steak 'n Shake burger, remember its Hoosier roots and the man who revived the iconic chain.

KELLEY AGRICULTURAL HISTORICAL MUSEUM

Injury This Bird, Go Directly to Jail

By Tim Bean

The Whooping Crane's Unnatural Extinction

Big, bold, and majestic, the whooping crane has edged closer to extinction than almost any American animal and, miraculously, survived (not really miraculously—droves of ornithologists, conservationists, volunteers, and even hunters provided the "miracle"). Hunters mowed down the whooping crane in the 1800s and early 1900s and, along with a loss of habitat (marsh lands across the central US), only 23 whooping cranes remained in 1941.

Standing over five feet tall, with a wingspan over seven feet, the whooping crane is hard to miss. Its distinctive call can carry for miles and individuals have been tracked for decades, including one male that lived over 26 years.

FLOCKING 101

Restoring the whooping crane to a thriving population took some time and a lot of trial-and-error. Despite the best efforts of conservationists, the whooping crane population only increased by approximately one bird a year from the 1950s to the late 1970s.

Real results didn't come to fruition until ornithologists tried some unorthodox methods of jumpstarting the population, including donning whooping crane outfits, leading flocks of flying whooping cranes in ultralight aircraft, and encouraging their nesting with sandhill cranes to learn proper "crane-ness".

Initially, conservation efforts utilizing the typical catch-and-release method of identifying and tracking individual birds in the wild, by simply photographing, measuring, and then banding the leg of the whooping crane. However, there is an inherent danger in capturing a five-foot tall bird weighing nearly twenty pounds, not only for the researchers, but for the bird itself. Because of the stress and danger of banding, voiceprint analysis became the preferred method of identifying and tracking individuals.

WHOOPING CRANE COSTUME (ON RIGHT)

Humans are by far the whooping crane's most dangerous threat, but several other species are known to prey on the crane's nest, including black bears, wolves, red foxes, and even mountain lions. When a nest is threatened, whooping cranes do not back down, and have been seen chasing off predators as large as wolves. Bobcats are the most dangerous predator of whooping cranes.

Bobcats use stealth to snatch chicks from the crane's nest. Because of this, bobcat populations near whooping crane nesting grounds are frequently moved to ensure the safety of juveniles.

Through these extreme conservation efforts, that number is currently up to approximately 800 cranes (including both those in the wild and in captivity).

Midwestern wildlife may be plentiful, but there are a handful of native and migratory species that state laws guard with extreme measures, largely because they totter at the brink of extinction. Penalties involving the whooping crane lean towards severe.

Categorized "endangered" under the criteria established by the Endangered Species Act of 1973, the whooping crane is in danger of extinction throughout most or all of its native range. Each state, including Indiana, has its own version of the ESA, but being "endangered" at the state-level typically refers to extinction in a localized range. The whooping crane is endangered *everywhere*. Injuring, killing, or simply harassing these birds would lead to a monsoon of criminal charges.

Penalties for killing, injuring, or simply harassing a whooping crane are stiff, and considered a federal crime, with a fine of up to $250,000 and six months in prison. In 2016, a Texas hunter shot and killed a whooping crane, paid a $25,000 fine and had his gun ownership rights suspended for five years (subsequently he decided to keep his guns anyway and was tossed in jail for a year to reconsider).

In the last ten years, four whooping cranes have been killed in Indiana, including one in 2017: a five-year-old female whooping crane killed by a high-powered rifle in the Goose Pond Fish and Wildlife Area in southern Indiana. The carefully tracked female had lost her chick during the 2016 breeding season and researchers hoped she would have been more successful in 2017. She wasn't, and the shooter was never caught.

Gimbel's Taught America How to Shop

By Mary Giorgio

In the 1840s, a Bavarian Jewish immigrant by the name of Adam Gimbel opened his first general store in Vincennes, Indiana. The Gimbel family would go on to become giants in the department store industry, eventually opening their famed store in New York City.

Adam Gimbel immigrated to America in 1835 and settled in New Orleans. After spending years traveling along the Mississippi River as a peddler, he settled in Vincennes and set up a general store along the Wabash River. The store would remain open for 40 years.

In 1887, **Bernard Gimbel** moved to Milwaukee, Wisconsin, to take advantage of its booming economy. There, he opened Gimbel's Brothers Department Store. The store sold everything from clothing and jewelry to furniture and housewares. Gimbel's soon became the leading retailer in Milwaukee, and its success prompted Adam's son, Isaac, to open a second location in

Philadelphia, Pennsylvania, in 1894. The store's headquarters later moved to Pennsylvania.

Adam's grandson, Bernard, is widely credited with developing some of Gimbel's most successful business practices. Bernard was born in Vincennes, Indiana, in 1885. In 1907, he graduated from the University of Pennsylvania and went to work for his family's company. Bernard's first role in the company was that of a shipping clerk. From there, he rose through the ranks, and by 1909, he had been promoted to Vice President. Bernard would later become the company's president.

In 1910, Bernard suggested that Gimbel's open a store in New York City. Winning his family's approval, Bernard quickly chose a site near Herald Square in Manhattan. The iconic New York

City location would later be portrayed in numerous films and television shows. Lucy Ricardo and Ethel Mertz shopped there (*I Love Lucy*). The store's fierce rivalry with its competitor, Macy's, was famously portrayed in *Miracle on 34th Street*.

In 1920, Bernard Gimbel pioneered a major first for the retail world. That November, the 1st Annual Gimbel's Thanksgiving Day Parade was held in downtown Philadelphia. The parade, designed to promote holiday shopping, began four years before Macy's held its first Thanksgiving Day Parade in New York City. Gimbel's annual parade continued until the company closed in 1987. It continues today under new sponsorship.

GIMBEL'S PARADE, 1975

The Gimbel's brand was synonymous with middle-class living and affordability. In the 1920s, the store expanded into the world of high-end retail shopping with the opening of its first Saks Fifth Avenue store. By 1930, the company had become the largest department store in the world with sales revenue topping $100 million a year.

When Gimbel's Department Store closed its doors in 1987, the company had been in business for 100 years. Its demise would foreshadow that of many other iconic American retailers. Although the chain has been closed for more than 30 years, it continues to be revered as an important part of America's retail history.

NEWSPAPER AD (1934)

The Most Dangerous Animal in North America? Bambi.

By Tim Bean

By the time you finish reading this, you may start rooting for the hunter instead of Disney's friendly fawn. Fair warning.

I promise that title's not clickbait. Whitetail deer, once commercially hunted down to a population of a few hundred thousand, has made a greater comeback than Muhammed Ali. But at a cost.

Why is your average, run-of-the-mill whitetail the most dangerous animal in the United States?

Bears (black, brown, and grizzly) kill 3 people per year in North America; dogs, 16 (although they bite about five million people per year). Mountain lions kill less than a person per year. Each year, deer-related accidents cause an average of 130 deaths, 29,000 injuries, and $1.2 billion in property damage.

There's Lyme disease. 300,000 Americans contract Lyme disease from ticks yearly, and large mammals like whitetails are an ideal carrier. Although attributing the percentage of those cases to deer would be impossible, Rhode Island's TickEncounter Index has demonstrated a direct relationship between increasing deer population and cases of Lyme disease in regions across the United States. The more deer, the more disease.

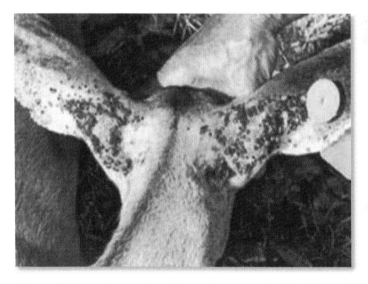

The efficient four-chambered stomach of whitetail deer allows them to eat just about any vegetable matter in reach, including poison ivy and toxic mushrooms. Experts at both foraging and survival, deer will also munch on baby birds, mice and even rats when handy. Their serene grazing might seem emblematic of the Great American Woodlands, but in densities of 20 deer or more per square mile, whitetail deer can exterminate a thriving forest as easily as a cloud of Agent Orange.

DEER VS. LANDSCAPING

Farmers regularly fall victim to the whitetail's voracious appetite. Deer lay siege to corn and fruit crops across the United States, and since an adult deer can easily jump a six-foot fence, farmers have to create costly barriers or attempt to exterminate the invading population, which is easier said than done. Ask any hunter (or landscaping enthusiast). Deer can be wily.

Deer, Everywhere

With 30 million deer (only 10 million below their pre-Colonial population) now living on the four million square miles of the United States, roughly 7.5 whitetail deer cover each square mile. That's not a comfortable margin from a tipping density of 20 deer per square mile.

Since settlers killed off the majority of the whitetail deer's natural predators, humans have taken their place, using the hunting industry

DEER ATTACKS HUNTER

and population control strategies regulated by the Department of Natural Resources. In essence, we replaced bears with shotguns and bureaucracy—and are not half as good at it.

Car accidents, disease, deforestation, crop destruction...Oh, and a whitetail deer might just outright attack you.

In May, 2019, three deer invaded an elderly woman's apartment in Decatur, Indiana, breaking through a large window and bounding inside. The deer, all does (female deers), kicked and leapt about the small apartment while she remained calm on her couch and called 911.

Police arrived and an officer immediately draped himself over her, shielding her from the dangerous, sharp kicks of the panicked animals. Although uninjured, the case demonstrates the risks inherent when worlds collide.

Direct aggression is not natural behavior for whitetail deer; their bodies are suited for flight and capable of sprinting at speeds over 45 mph. Even the namesake part of their anatomy—the white tail—is used to warn others of a possible threat.

If deer feel flight is impossible, they won't hesitate to turn on a human with lithe, powerful legs capable of fracturing a human skull. As deer populations grow more comfortable with humans and their territory overlaps ours, dangerous and possibly fatal encounters will increase.

That goes doubly true for does carrying for their young, which may see a human's presence as a direct threat to her fawns. In that case...run. Never mess with a mommy.

Bucks are rarely as protectively aggressive, except for those few, furious weeks of rut in the autumn. At that time all bets are off. During rut, a mature buck boils with two hundred pounds of anxious muscle, a need to fight, and sports head-spears worn to a dull shine—few animals are as dangerous and unpredictable as a buck during rut.

This is all fine and good, but have deer honestly ever attacked or killed anyone?

~On June 4th, 2019, an aggressive blacktail doe stomped a family dog to death and chased several residents from their porches and patios into their homes. This has gone on for weeks.

~In April, 2019, a pet deer in Australia gored his owner of six years to death during a feeding. When the fatally-injured man's wife came to help her husband, the deer attacked her as well. The woman barely survived after being airlifted to a nearby hospital.

~In 2011, an injured buck in Fort Wayne, Indiana, stabbed an approaching hunter through the liver, killing him.

~In 2006, a buck attacked a fisherman at a secluded reservoir in North Texas. The fisherman received several deep cuts and an impaled hand. The fisherman's son luckily stepped in and killed the deer. The attack was unprovoked, except that it occurred during the rut.

Indiana, Welcome to Tornado Alley

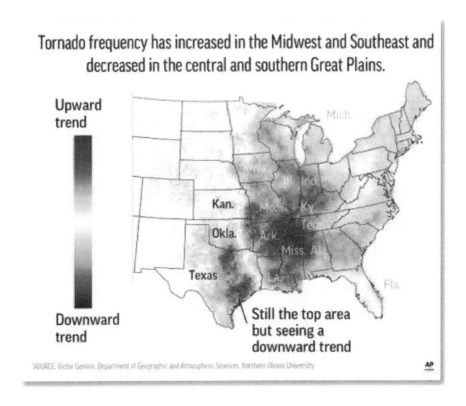

Tornado frequency has increased in the Midwest and Southeast and decreased in the central and southern Great Plains.

Upward trend

Downward trend

Kan.

Okla.

Texas

Mich.

Ind.

Ky.

Ark.

Miss.

Fla.

Still the top area but seeing a downward trend

SOURCE: Victor Gensini, Department of Geographic and Atmospheric Sciences, Northern Illinois University

AP

By Tim Bean

Indiana, we just received one of the least-welcome invitations in our history, and we can't turn it down.

Once upon a time, Indiana only had a seasonal place in Tornado Alley, typically in the spring, when warm equatorial air meets frigid arctic air in a rolling turmoil. Since the term and its borders shift with annual weather trends, Indiana was sometimes included, sometimes not. Not anymore.

155

In 2016, Purdue meteorologists and climatologists compared two sets of tornado data: 1954-1983 and 1983-2013. They concluded that the center of tornado activity, once firmly in Oklahoma, has now shifted to Alabama. With the center goes the "alley", and while Indiana had once been on its fringe, it is now the center of the northern tip.

Double-Checking the Data

Being scientific scientists, Purdue had to verify the data firsthand. Researchers went into the field, traveling to Tornado Alley's new center in Alabama. In the spring of 2016 and 2017, they used sensitive radar systems and a mobile station to analyze thousands of passing storms, squeezing a wealth of data on precipitation, pressure, wind speed, and temperature, filling up scores up hard drives. Then they began the arduous task of deciphering it.

In fact, Purdue climatologists are still combing through the data, but it's already clear that the first study has been confirmed: Tornado Alley HAS moved. The cause is most likely climate change, but given the climate denialism rampant in today's public and private spheres, Purdue's climatologists are not formally announcing that conclusion until the analysis is complete, published, and peer-reviewed...because they're good scientists.

What does this mean for Hoosiers?

That's not so clear. It doesn't mean Indiana will suddenly be swarmed with out-of-state tornadoes, taking our jobs and taxes. But it may mean tornadoes will be harder to predict across the state and harder to track, and their intensity may increase. That's a lot of *mays*, I know, but it's a reality that we're only beginning to accept. Weather is fickle. Especially Indiana weather.

The news is not all bad. According to the National Weather Service, the number of fatalities has decreased since 1950, largely because of improvements in weather tracking technology and warning systems. Tornadoes and weather-related hazards are bipartisan concerns, and legislative funding outcries come less frequently. We all agree tornadoes aren't pretty from the inside.

Hoosiers may love watching tornadoes—it's in our cultural blood —but that doesn't mean we trust them.

Stay safe, Indiana.

The Indiana Bridge Stolen a Pound at a Time

ca. 1912 Photo. Source: 1912 Great Lakes Dredge and Dock Company Brochure

By Tim Bean

Some saw the Monon bridge as a decaying symbol of Hammond's proud industrial past. Kenneth Morrison saw it as tens of thousands of dollars in valuable scrap iron, wasting away on the edge of the Grand Calumet.

The Hammond Monon Bridge had once been a fixture Hammond's ever-growing industries, with thousands of tons of imports and exports rambling over its Warren-truss design. The Monon Bridge also provided much of the railroad service for Hammond's meatpacking companies in the early 1900s, with some of the earliest refrigerated railcars likely crossing the river there.

Built in 1909, various railroad lines purchased and utilized the iron bridge for eight decades, but time, use, and the elements had weakened the metal. Minor fixes and patching became so frequent that CSX Transportation, its final owner, wanted to wash its hands of the Hammond-Monon Bridge.

In the 1980s, the company stopped using the bridge and, instead, decided to donate it to the city, for preservation, for scrap, for posterity (mostly for the tax write-off).

Hammond wasn't interested and the city's official stance was "no comment." CSX Transportation offered it again, and again, to the city, and it wasn't until 1987 that the city grudgingly accepted the donated bridge.

Rain or shine, through sweltering summers and record-setting winters, the Hammond Monon Bridge sat unused and rotting into a tangled mass of old iron. Only graffiti artists were interested in her anymore.

KENNETH MORRISON

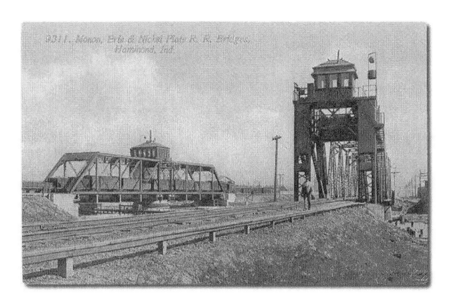

In 1991, a Whiting scrap metal dealer named Kenneth Morrison, owner of T & K Metals, saw the potential value in the old bridge, and offered to buy the antique bridge from Hammond. Hammond officials said no. Thirteen years passed, with no move on the city to repair, restore, or remove the bridge.

For the owner of a small business, watching good metal (and money) sitting and rotting at the riverside must have been torture. He approached the city yet again: kill two birds with one stone, they'd have cash in hand for the sale of the bridge, and be rid of an aging and potential dangerous eyesore.

Nah, said Hammond.

In December of 2014, Morrison brought a small crew of workers to the bridge, which was only a few blocks away from the Hammond courthouse. Using metal cutters and portable torches, Morrison began slicing up the metal into transportable chunks. Well-versed in the jungles of red tape involving scrap purchases, he juggled lie after lie to officials, his workers, and those buying the scrap metal.

It wasn't until late January of 2015 that Hammond discovered the crime. By that time, Morrison had chopped up half the bridge, hauling the old iron to Illinois scrapyards, and made about $14,000 for his efforts.

It was a bold crime. Morrison used an entire crew, in broad daylight, and wallpapered the entire activity with lies. Even when Hammond ordered him to cease dismantling the bridge, he continued for several days. In his words, the bridge was nothing more than a "shipwreck" abandoned by the city, and its contents were fair game.

THE BRIDGE SITE TODAY

The hammer came down. Since Morrison removed the bridge in Indiana and sold the allegedly stolen metal in Illinois, crossing state lines, it became a federal crime, involving the FBI. In the process of removing the metal, Morrison's workers had left chunks of metal and railroad timber in the Grand Calumet, so the Indiana Department of Environmental Management investigated. And the EPA joined in for good measure.

Hammond itself had it out for Morrison, seemingly taking his "overzealous entrepreneurial spirit" personally. Interstate transportation of stolen goods. As said, the hammer came down, but has yet to land.

Hammond did not file its deed to the bridge, which was ceded to the city in 1987, until *after* charging Morrison. This glaring "coincidence" has turned the battle of the now-vanished Hammond Monon Bridge into a mess. Trying to follow his trial is like trying to follow a tennis match in the dark. An expert in scrap metal acquisition, Morrison knows his way around the legal pitfalls of the process and his successful business has allowed him to continue the fight for years.

His chief argument, and that of his lawyers, is that this should be a civil case, not a criminal one. Hammond's interest in pursuing criminal charges are entirely punitive, an assessment that seems more and more likely as this case drags out.

In January of this year, Morrison came back at Hammond yet again, requesting a new trial. According to his lawyers, Hammond did not demonstrate clear ownership of the bridge, and Morrison deserves to be acquitted and retried.

UFO over Southern Indiana?

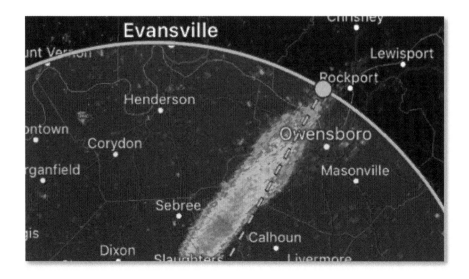

By Tim Bean

On the afternoon of December 11th, 2018, a large blob materialized over southern Illinois, slid across the horn of southern Indiana into Kentucky and finally vanished over Tennessee. Soon after, Kentucky's National Weather Service posted a radar-tracking video of the mysterious shape.

Evansville meteorologist Wayne Hart decided the blob, which lasted about ten hours and drifted hundreds of miles, was worth some phone calls, and hours after the original post, he took to Twitter

Chaff is made from a variety of reflective materials, but all has the same purpose: as a countermeasure to confuse radar systems.

Since World War II, aviators have used to chaff to disguise clandestine military aircraft and weaponry.

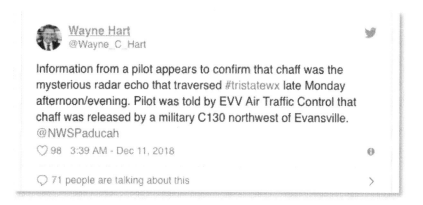

Unlike the material on a modern stealth aircraft, which renders it invisible to aircraft, chaff acts more like a smokescreen, displaying a massive, globular target. Chaff used during World War II was simply strips of aluminum foil, and in that time, it hasn't changed much.

But why release it over Illinois and Indiana in the middle of the day?

Apparently, a C-130 Hercules, one of the military's 100-foot long workhorse transport planes (and the longest continuously manufactured plane in military history at 60 years), dropped a load of chaff during an unannounced military exercise over Illinois.

That was as specific as anyone would get. Nothing to see here.

C-130

The story threaded its way through the conspiracy corridors of Twitter almost immediately and blew up. From which military airfield did the C-130 originate? No Indiana-based plane had chaff in the air at the time. How did it linger for ten hours and float hundreds of miles? Was it a new, classified material? Why was it released at 10,000 feet, an oddly-low altitude for a military plane?

Answers flooded in from the craziest corners of the United States. New, state-of-the-art aircraft. Terrorists. Aliens. Military coverups. Aliens. Incompetent radar operators. Incompetent weathermen. Tumbling spacecraft. Contrails and vaccine connections and stratospheric aerosol injections, oh my!

And aliens.

The US military knows that in the absence of disclosure, the vacuum is filled by crackpots, so the Air National Guard sighed, shrugged, and graciously filled in the blanks, offering a tale marginally less interesting than aliens with anal probes.

A C-130 Hercules out of West Virginia crossed Illinois after participating in an exercise on the West Coast. Before landing in West Virginia, it needed to eject its chaff cartridges as a safety precaution, and was given permission to do so at a low altitude over Illinois, minimizing any interference with civilian aircraft.

So what have we learned from this article?

We learned a little about C-130s and radar-masking chaff.

We also learned that when it comes to the comings and goings of the military, speculation is about as effective as unclogging a toilet with a house cat.

Seymour Mastodon Finds Home at Indiana State Museum

By Tim Bean

The Indiana State Museum is now the proud recipient of a 12,000 pound mastodon. Or at least the bones of one.

In early April this year, workers installing a sewer line through a Seymour farm unearthed a cache of massive bones and reported the discovery to Indiana's DNR, who then contacted the farm's owners, the Nehrt-Schepman Family. Surprised, owner Joe Schepman thought it was fuss over nothing at first, and "it's a chicken bone or cow bone or something like that"...until he saw the bones for himself.

The family contacted the Indiana State Museum, which immediately sent Ron Richards, senior research curator of paleobiology, who happily confirmed the find as belonging to a

167

mastodon, a family of megafauna ("big animals") which had once roamed across North and Central America thousands of years ago.

These seven bones—remnants of limbs, a tusk and skull among them—represent a unique find in southern Indiana. The nutrient-rich soil of the southern half of the Hoosier state typically consumes animal remains quickly, leaving little behind. Additionally, Lake Chicago and the Huron-Erie Ice, massive glaciers that flattened northern Indiana during the last Ice Age (and would melt to become the Great Lakes), did not extend below Indianapolis, a region that may have been uncomfortable warm for the heavily-furred mastodon.

After dubbing the discovery "Alfred", the family recently donated the bones to the Indiana State Museum, which will spend the next year carefully examining and preserving the specimen. The museum promises to offer frequent updates on "Alfred", including the possibility of a future exhibition featuring this new celebrity of southern Indiana megafauna.

Thanks to the largesse of the Nehrt-Schepman family, museum staff will also search the "Alfred" discovery site. Mastodons lived in herds, making the piece of Seymour farmland a prime candidate for future discoveries.

The Indiana State Museum contains the most diverse collection of mammoth and mastodon bones in the Midwest, and is one of the leading research centers for mastodon studies in the United States. Although frequently used interchangeably, mastodons and mammoths were genetically-diverse species, with mastodons thriving in North and Central America.

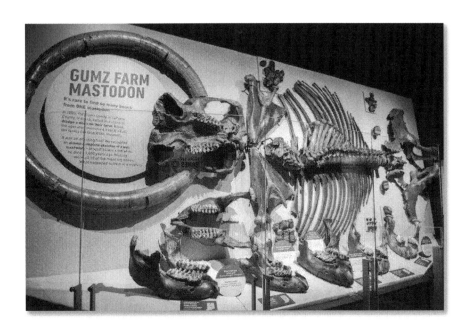

Like many indigenous megafauna, mastodons and mammoths died out around 12,000 years ago at the beginning of the Holocene extinction*, largely from overhunting by early homo sapiens (although isolated populations of mammoths limped on until as recently as 1650 BC, after the Great Pyramids of Giza were constructed). Because of human responsibility in their extinction, viable DNA specimens, and a physiological similarity to modern elephants, mastodons and mammoths remain a possibility for "genetic de-extinction."

In other words, pulling a "Jurassic Park."

*The Holocene extinction, also known as the Sixth Extinction, began approx. 12,000 years ago and still continues today: scientists define it as the thousands of plant and animal species forced into extinction by human activity...including the American mastodon.

The Complex History of the Governor's Mansion(s)

A vintage postcard image shows the Indiana governor's residence in Corydon. The house no longer stands.

By Mary Giorgio

Drive down Meridian Street in Indianapolis, and you will pass the imposing residence of the governor of Indiana, aptly named the Indiana Governor's Residence. Many people don't realize this historic mansion is not the original home or location of the Indiana governor's residence.

In the 1820s, Indiana's capital had recently moved from Corydon to Indianapolis, and the governor needed an official residence. The Indiana legislature voted to spend $4,000 to build a home for its governor and began the search for an ideal location, finally deciding on the then-empty Monument Circle at the city's center.

Completed in 1829, the total cost of the project was over budget at $6,500. The home was two stories with a yellow brick exterior. It was set six feet off the ground, with an imposing staircase to the front door.

Inside, the home was a disaster. The interior was drafty and poorly laid-out. Each floor was broken into four large rooms with removable walls, so that rooms could easily be enlarged for gatherings. Details important to most families were omitted. For example, there was no kitchen in the home.

The mansion did feature a magnificent outdoor space. A rooftop patio allowed residents to enjoy nice weather. Gardens and a fence completed the landscape. Once completed, Governor James Brown Ray brought his wife to see the home. She was horrified and refused to live there. Her biggest complaint was the location.

SKETCH OF 1st GOVERNOR'S MANSION

Mrs. Ray immediately noticed that the home's position at the center of the city would afford her family no privacy. She was said to have panicked at the thought of the city's residents gawking at the family's laundry hanging out to dry.

Future first ladies of Indiana echoed Mrs. Ray's sentiments. In the end, the home was never used as a governor's residence. Instead, the Supreme Court of Indiana used the home as office space. The Indiana State Library was temporarily located there during construction of a new building. The basement was even used as a kindergarten.

THE SECOND "MANSION"...

By 1851, the first mansion had fallen into disrepair. It was sold at auction in 1857 and torn down. Without the imposing brick structure, the circle became an empty expanse of land, where cows grazed and pigs wandered. Neighborhood children often played on the muddy site.

Meanwhile, the state tried to secure a different residence for its governor. A two-story brick mansion at the northwest corner of Illinois and Market Street was acquired in 1839. The first governor to occupy the home was David Wallace.

Unfortunately, a plague of illnesses suffered by subsequent governors and their wives led to the conclusion that the mansion was making its residents sick. One governor died shortly after leaving office. Two governors' wives died in the mansion. A third governor's wife was sick the entire time she lived there.

Mansion Down

In 1863, Governor Oliver P. Morton evacuated his family from the mansion in an attempt to remedy their poor health. The home was sold by the legislature in 1865. It was torn down and later replaced by the Cyclorama building. Today it is home to a bus terminal.

Although the original governors' mansion on the circle was never occupied by an Indiana governor, it remained an important location for early state government operations. A suitable permanent home was eventually acquired on Meridian St. Today, Monument Circle continues to be the heart of downtown Indianapolis.

A sincere thank you to astute reader Wendy Haines for her keen eye in spotting a couple historical errors.

CURRENT OFFICIAL RESIDENCE

The Problem with Potholes

By Tim Bean

*Disclaimer: I do not work for the DOT or for any entity involved in road or highway repair. I am just a fan of fixing things right the first time.

Billions of Dollars, Thousands of Lives

According to the American Automobile Association (AAA), potholes cost American drivers approximately $3 billion a year, and are involved in over 3,000 fatalities. That's not a problem, that's a plague.

Fixing the pothole problem on America's roads isn't as easy as most people think, and it's a problem that comes back year after year. Simply filling in potholes is not enough of a solution, but to understand the magnitude of the problem, we have to look what causes these car craters and methods used to repair them.

Before pointing our righteous fingers in the quick-blame game, we should remember that the men and women repairing these potholes are men and women, with lives, homes, and health. They are out there pouring hot asphalt into these craters in 100 degree summer weather and tossing shovels of stinking rock and tar on them in below-freezing winters.

Whether or not the paycheck is nice isn't the question; it's a hard job for anyone to do. We should also remember that asphalt is a proven carcinogen, made even more dangerous when heated, and the men and women of the DOT are spending their entire day working with it.

How about tossing them a shovelful of empathy?

Pothole Problem: From Bad to Worse

Our ever-increasing pothole problem shouldn't be a surprise to anyone. Much of the state and county road system in the United States is around 100 years old. Today, 222 million people in the United States possess driver's licenses; that's more than twice the total number of US citizens when most of roads were made. Our surprise shouldn't be that the roads are falling apart but that they have lasted this long!

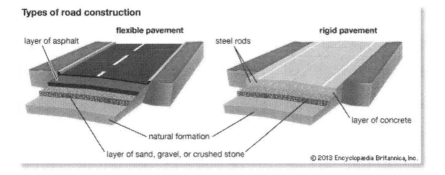

Types of road construction

flexible pavement · rigid pavement

layer of asphalt · steel rods

layer of concrete

natural formation

layer of sand, gravel, or crushed stone

© 2013 Encyclopædia Britannica, Inc.

Our interstate highway system largely sprang out of the Eisenhower-era of the 1950s. On these roads, contractors used mostly concrete, not asphalt, and utilized advanced construction techniques that allowed stronger surfaces with better drainage. Potholes aren't rare, but they're not nearly as common.

State and county roads, however, are made of asphalt, a sticky and flexible mixture of petroleum aggregate. 70% of the world's asphalt is used in road construction, and can be applied either cold or hot. Asphalt has many advantages as a construction material. It's relatively cheap and abundant, and can be easily cut

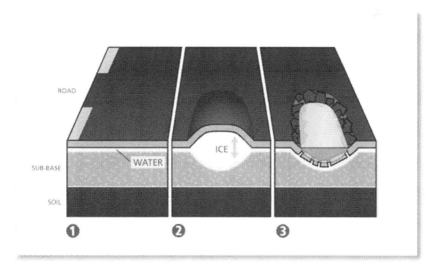

ROAD

SUB-BASE

SOIL

WATER

ICE

❶ ❷ ❸

through and removed if workers needed to access areas below ground (such as a sewer system). Since it is semi-viscous, it lends itself to virtually any surface contour as well.

That flexibility has a cost. If roads have poor drainage, either from construction errors or disrepair, water pools beneath the asphalt, between the road and sub-base. In warmer climates this isn't as heavy a concern for roads, which is why asphalt in the subtropical climates of the United States tend to last longer.

But in temperate climates, such as those of Indiana, water freezes every year. Freezes and thaws, freezes and thaws. In terms of erosion, nothing on Earth is more destructive than water, and its property of expanding and contracting during this process is water at its most destructive.

ALLIGATORING

As illustrated in the above graphic (and the image below) given enough expansion and contraction, asphalt will show the telltale signs of subsidence in the sub-base, manifesting on the surface as alligator-cracking or *alligatoring*, for its cosmetic similarity to the skin of a alligator. No matter the name, it ultimately means road surface failure.

Road crews can repair these cracks, but it's a temporary measure at best. At worst, it's a waste of time. No matter how it's repaired, the end result will be a pothole, and the only solution is cutting through the damaged surface, removing the chunks of hardened asphalt, assessing the sub-base condition, and repairing the fault completely.

Honestly, for a problem area that might last for months or even years longer, this is not typically a priority, since larger, more potholes are likely in need of repair.

COLD PATCH ASPHALT

Asphalt used in road repair is not exactly the same as that which you'd buy at a home improvement store. Cold patch asphalt, sold in buckets or bags on the shelves of Home Depot or Lowe's, can be used to fill virtually any pothole, but most DIYers take its ease-of-use for granted. Long-term, heavy-use repairs cannot be performed in the same way as driveway repairs (although crews do use cold patch asphalt in certain circumstances).

These are the repairs you WON'T do at home.

Throw-and-roll

The least expensive and most common repair, this is the method most often used by crews not because of its durability but its efficiency. Crews can roll down the length of a badly-damaged road, leaving it partially open for traffic flow, and repair a large number of potholes in a short time.

However, throw-and-roll fixes rarely last long, and it's common to see the same hole fixed two or times in the same year, especially in areas of heavy traffic. It's also the most common repair conducted in dangerously cold or hot weather.

Workers "throw" asphalt into the hole, sometimes removing loose material but often leaving broken asphalt and standing water.

The hole is filled and then overfilled, and then another vehicle (or the same one) compacts the patch with its tires until there's a slight crown on the surface, usually no more than a 1/4 to 3/8 of an inch, to allow for future subsidence.

Semi-permanent repairs

If weather or schedules allow better repairs, crews can supplement throw-and-roll repairs with several further steps. First, before filling, any water or debris is completely removed from the pothole. Next, a pavement saw slices through the asphalt, neatly squaring off its jagged edges.

After being filled, the hole is flattened using a vibratory-plate compactor, sort of the heavy-duty version of a handheld tamper. This allows the asphalt aggregate to seal and settle, leaving behind a firm surface.

Spray Injection Repairs

Another excellent semi-permanent repair are spray injectors, which allow crews to clear, clean, and fill potholes with a single tool. Spraying the aggregate into the pothole, versus simple shoveling it in, also allows the new asphalt to fill tiny crevices that might otherwise cause the pothole to reappear.

This method's also removes the step of compacting the asphalt, since the action of spraying it achieves the same end. The downside? Spray injecting trucks cost big bucks, and need frequent maintenance.

The Finishing Touch: Edge Sealing

The last step in any pothole repair is edge sealing. Faults are most likely to appear at the edge of a pothole, which is where water will seep in, and where a vehicle's tires strike with the most direct force against a smaller surface.

After a pothole dries, a crew can return and use a thin mixture of hot asphalt to seal these edges, adding strength and increased water resistance to a repair. Although it's time consuming, it's the step that transforms a repair that last a year to one that lasts several years. In terms of money and man-hours, that's a big difference.

A final note on repairs: notice I don't include "permanent" in this? That's because permanent repairs don't really exist when it comes to potholes. The moisture that caused the damage in the first place is likely still there and unless the entire surface, sub-base and drainage system is repaired, the pothole will eventually return.

Solving the Pothole Crisis?

Unless we decide to completely overhaul our roads nationwide, a fiscally and logistical impossibility, the only real solution is funding and patience. For those who have suffered vehicular damage or worse because of potholes, this provides little satisfaction, but it's the only viable one.

In order for crews to repair a pothole right the first time, we have to contend with detours and slow-moving traffic. The irony is obvious, considering the least patient human on Earth is one which is stuck in traffic. Ironic or not, that's reality.

Campaigns to allocate more workers, crews, or funds toward pothole repair is a possibility, but when that means higher taxes, American citizens tend to get antsy. We're sensitive about taxation; it's in our cultural blood, so to speak.

So that leaves patience. Which hardly seems like a solution at all.

Indiana's Historic Roberts Settlement

By Mary Giorgio

In 1835, one of Indiana's oldest African-American settlements was founded just north of Indianapolis in Hamilton County. Attracted by the low cost of fertile farmland, three men—Hansel Roberts, Elijah Roberts, and Micajah Walden—purchased farmland and founded a community of free African-Americans. Roberts Settlement would go on to become famous for its success and prosperity.

Most of these settlers came from North Carolina and Virginia, and many members of the community had been slaves on the same plantation, accounting for the fact that the majority of early residents to the settlement shared the surname Roberts.

The Roberts settlers hoped the move to Indiana would provide them with opportunities for economic prosperity, good education, and religious freedom. They chose to build their community in northern Hamilton County because there was an abundance of high-quality, low-cost farmland.

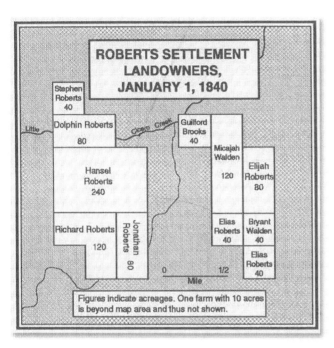

Their nearest neighbors were members of the Quaker and Wesleyan faiths, both of which were known for their abolitionist leanings and tolerance of free African-American communities. Indeed, the Roberts Settlement quickly formed a beneficial relationship with their neighbors in both trade and friendship.

By 1838, members of the settlement owned 900 acres of farmland. Their hard work paid off. The community erected a church and school in 1847, along with numerous shops and small businesses. With the coming of the railroad in the 1850s, markets for the community's farm goods. By 1858, community members had accumulated enough wealth to build a new church.

At the peak of their economic success in the late 1800s, the Roberts Settlement owned 1,700 acres of land and had over 250 residents. The community began to decline in the early 1900s, as farmland became increasingly hard to purchase at an affordable price. The decline in affordable land coincided with the development of factories in nearby Kokomo and Noblesville. Many residents moved away to take jobs in these factories.

Today, descendants of the original Roberts settlers live all over the country.

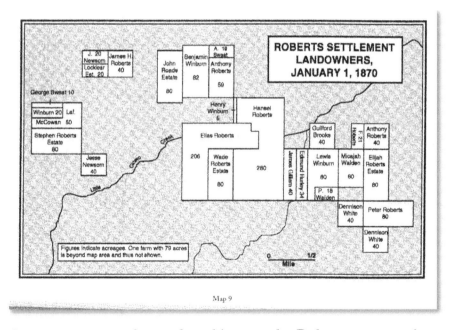

Map 9

As a testament to the profound impact the Roberts community had on its residents and their descendants, an annual gathering occurs on the weekend nearest to July 4th. These homecomings have been taking place since 1925. Each year, descendants turn out to reconnect and pay tribute to the accomplishments of their ancestors.

The community's historic church has been preserved and features prominently in these reunions. The original cemetery still stands, along with a few old farmhouses. In 2016, the Indiana Historical Bureau erected a historic marker commemorating the community's origins.

While little remains of the original community, the Roberts Settlement continues its legacy as one of the first successful African American communities in Indiana. Surviving and prospering for generations, Roberts Settlement served as a model and inspiration for other African-American communities across Indiana and the Midwest.

ROBERTS CHAPEL TODAY

When Indianapolis Saved the Life of a President

By Tim Bean

President Theodore Roosevelt dedicated his life to conquering the ghost of his sickly childhood...but as he stood on Monument Circle before a sea of supporters, the infection boiling in his wounded leg had reduced him to limping agony.

Less than three weeks earlier, as his presidential entourage had trotted down a Massachusetts street, a speeding electric trolley had slammed into his open carriage, killing Secret Service Agent William Craig and flinging Roosevelt from the carriage to the pavement. As usual, Roosevelt dismissed the few cuts and scraps, looking only to the well-being of others.

Only a single wound, a shallow but lengthy laceration down his left leg, caused him any lasting pain, but for a veteran solider and consummate outdoorsman, such a wound was a trifle. It would turn out to be life-threatening.

Theodore Roosevelt Collection, Harvard College Library

CARRIAGE AFTER ACCIDENT

The tireless Teddy Roosevelt commenced with a speaking tour of the Midwest, anxious to support his fellow Republicans in an upcoming race as well as legitimize his newborn presidency. Only a year earlier, his predecessor, President William McKinley, died from septicemia after an (ultimately successful) assassination attempt.

As his tour took him through the Midwest and then to the Hoosier State, the wound on his leg grew hot, swollen and painful to the touch. When out of the public eye, President Roosevelt rested in a wheelchair, but even this brought him little relief. Hot needles of infection pierced every step, and yellow pus curdled beneath the wound's feverish skin.

His legendary endurance gave out in Indianapolis, when the crowd notice the boisterous young president wince repeatedly during his impassioned speech.

In 1902, before the advent of antibiotics, infections were deadly business. If left untreated, they could quickly turn into blood poisoning (sepsis or septicemia), leading to a long and agonizingly-painful death. No steely resolve could save Roosevelt, and his staff hurried him to emergency surgery at St. Vincent's Hospital in Indianapolis.

Word of Roosevelt's illness quickly spread, and when news of possible blood poisoning leaked, hundreds of solemn onlookers stood vigil outside the Roman-Catholic hospital. They remembered well the condition that had taken McKinley.

191

For the second time in a year, the American public waited for news of another president's death.

Polite to a fault, Roosevelt apologized to the hospital staff for their troubles as he was carried to surgery. The surgeon, Dr. John Oliver, readied instruments to lance and clean the leg infection, a simple but lengthy procedure. Given the wound's size and the president's observed pain, Dr. Oliver strongly suggested a general anesthetic, but Roosevelt refused, accepting only a local anesthetic in his leg.

ST. VINCENT'S, EARLY 1900s

For an hour, the doctor pressed, cleaned and drained the wound, kneading the raw, infected nerves in Roosevelt's leg. No local anesthetic could kill the pain, only dull it, but the president weathered it bravely, clutching his hands behind his head, clamping his teeth, and screwing his eyes shut. He never made a peep.

Only days later, he was back in Washington D.C., and recuperated quickly from the near-death experience more charismatic and energetic than ever. The American public understandably celebrated, and the near loss boosted national affection. Roosevelt would go on and mold the United States from an industrious but isolated nation to a world superpower and economic leader.

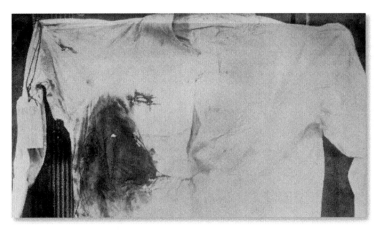

ROOSEVELT'S SHIRT AFTER ATTEMPT

A decade later, President Theodore Roosevelt would survive an assassination attempt, four years after he left office and during his campaign as delegate for the Progressive Party. An assassin (later judged insane) fired a .38 caliber revolver directly at Roosevelt's chest as the president exited a restaurant in Milwaukee. According to the assassin, the ghost of McKinley had ordered it.

Roosevelt fell back but immediately sprang to his feet and ordered the furious crowd to unhand the would-be assassin.

Police arrested him, and the president did not leave until he ensured police had proper custody, and the crowd would cause the assassin no harm.

Using his knowledge as a soldier and hunter, Roosevelt decided the wound was only superficial, and he decided to give his speech...instead of first seeing a doctor. He did, with a patch of blood growing like a corsage on his shirt.

The Short Life of the White City Amusement Park

By Mary Giorgio

*Named the "White City" for its Combination of White Stucco and Streetlights

At the 1893 World's Columbian Exposition, visitors were treated to novel entertainment in the form of an amusement park. Following the Exposition, amusement parks began cropping up across the United States. Indianapolis got three – Riverside Amusement Park, Wonderland, and White City Amusement Park.

Located in Broad Ripple, the White City Amusement Park opened on May 26, 1906. The park sat at the end of a streetcar line, making it easily accessible to residents of Indianapolis, for a cost of twenty centers per person.

Opening Indianapolis

On opening day, the park gained local attention by hiring an airship, the *White Eagle*, to hover over the park. It dropped money orders that could be redeemed at the Indianapolis Star news office.

White City featured rides, live entertainment, and a bandstand. Visitors flocked to the park's merry-go-round, roller coasters, and funhouse. Entertainment included marching bands, acrobats, and vaudeville shows. Exhibits such as "Fighting the Flames," a mock firefighting display, were also very popular. Restaurants, a baseball diamond, even a place for roller skating and dancing.

WHITE EAGLE

Competitive Spectacles

All three area parks opened to great fanfare, but owners realized almost immediately that three parks with similar offerings were not sustainable in such proximity. White City tried to beat out its rivals by innovating. They worked to attract the best talent for live entertainment. In 1907, the park added a billiard hall, a model

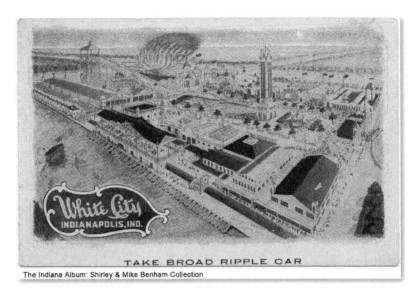

city, and an exhibit titled "Paris by Night" to distinguish itself from competitors.

Biggest. Pool. Ever.

In 1908, White City announced the opening of its newest attraction – the largest swimming pool in the world. The pool was dug from two acres of land and measured 500 feet by 250 feet. It was set to open on June 27, 1908. The night before the big grand opening, tragedy struck at the park. A fire started in the Mystic Cave exhibit, and soon it had spread across park grounds. The new pool was the only area that didn't burn to the ground.

Rebuilding

Unfortunately, most of the park was uninsured. Owners couldn't afford to rebuild. The park sat vacant for three years before it was finally purchased by the Union Traction Company of Indiana. Shortly thereafter, the park reopened. Under new ownership, the pool became one of the main attractions. A dance hall, dining hall, and playground rounded out the new park's offerings.

The pool gained national attention. In 1922, the park hosted a national swimming competition. In 1924, Olympic tryouts were conducted there.

The Park Site Today

FORMER WHITE CITY SITE, NOW BROAD RIPPLE PARK

In May 1922, the White City Amusement Park was sold to the Broad Ripple Amusement Park Association, and the park was renamed the Broad Ripple Amusement Park. Then, in 1945, it changed hands again. The park was purchased by the City of Indianapolis and turned into a public park. The pool was filled in.

An End of an Era

Today, the era of amusement park entertainment in Indianapolis is a distant memory. All that remains of the White City's past is a historic carousel installed at the Children's Museum of Indianapolis. Dating to about 1917, the carousel has been a fixture at the museum since the 1960s.

President W. H. Harrison's Historic Grouseland

By Mary Giorgio

Fans of the TV sitcom, *Parks and Recreation*, might recall an episode featuring Grouseland, home of the 9th President of the United States. Located in Vincennes, Indiana, Grouseland played a prominent role in the early history of Indiana. Today, it is a museum honoring the legacy of its first owner, William Henry Harrison.

Harrison was born in Virginia in 1773. He came from a prominent family, and Harrison's father was one of the signers of the Declaration of Independence.

As a young man, Harrison studied medicine. Rather than becoming a doctor, he decided to join the military. In 1791, Harrison received an officer's commission to the Army and was assigned to the Northwest Territory. After three years of service, he resigned his commission to become secretary of the territory. He also served as its first representative to Congress.

In 1800, Harrison was appointed governor of the new Indiana Territory. The capital city was established at Vincennes. Harrison moved his family there. He purchased 300 acres of land, which the family aptly named Grouseland after the many birds that frequented the area.

In 1804, the Harrison family moved into their newly constructed Federal-style home. It was the first all-brick home built in Indiana. In addition to housing his family, Harrison used the home to conduct territorial business. He hosted many important meetings in what became known as the "Council Chamber."

COUNCIL CHAMBER

Harrison's famed meeting with Native American leader
Tecumseh took place in this room. Tecumseh had traveled to
Vincennes to warn Harrison that he would lead a war against the
territorial army if they continued to take land from Native
American tribes.

In 1811, Harrison led territorial troops to confront Tecumseh at
his encampment in Prophetstown, Indiana. Harrison's men
claimed victory in the battle, which became known as the Battle
of Tippecanoe. One year later, Harrison resigned his position as
governor to return to military service. He fought in the War of
1812.

GENERAL HARRISON.

At the war's conclusion, the Harrison family abandoned
Grouseland for North Bend, Ohio. Harrison became active in
politics, winning seats in the Ohio House and Senate. He later
served as a representative to Congress. In 1840, Harrison was
tapped by the Whig party to run for president. He campaigned as

a war hero, running the first modern presidential campaign in history, traveling around the country to meet voters ahead of the election.

One month after his inauguration, Harrison was dead following a mysterious illness long thought to be pneumonia. Today, he is remembered as the shortest serving president in US history.

After the Harrison family moved to Ohio, Grouseland slowly fell into disrepair. In 1909, it was saved from demolition by a local chapter of the Daughters of the American Revolution. The women restored the home and eventually turned it into a museum. Today Grouseland is a National Historic Landmark.

Delicious, Delectable, and Disgusting Indiana Dishes

By Tim Bean

We love to eat, and what's wrong with that?

Indiana earned the title "Crossroads of America" for the tangle of highways that criss-crossed the state, but that hodgepodge of cultural traffic brought with it a hodgepodge of food fancies.

This list is by no means definitive, and I fully expect someone to read it and curse me for forgetting an essential dish. I apologize in advance. I have been a Hoosier since birth and did my best.

Sugar Cream Pie

This first dish is the most obvious, because it is the official pie of the Hoosier state. There's a thousand varieties and as many

recipes...so instead of providing a recipe, I'll only mention Wick's Pies in Winchester, Indiana, which sells 750,000 sugar cream pies a year. If they sell that many pies, chances are they know how to make them better than anyone.

Breaded Pork Tenderloin Sandwich

Take a lean(-ish) cut of pork and run it through a tenderizer a half-dozen times. Bread it, fry it, and slap it between two buns with a generous glob of mayonnaise, onions, some pickles and lettuce...Is that really all there is to it? Thankfully, no.

This crispy sandwich should be the size of a dinner plate to earn a Hoosier's appreciation. If you're too busy to cook, then try one at its source: Nick's Kitchen in Huntington, Indiana, is recognized as the first to serve this hulk of a meal. Order one for lunch. By the time dinner rolls around, you might have it finished.

Hoosier Chili

Don't be surprised if you spot a Hoosier or Buckeye pouring this concoction over some spaghetti or macaroni. The biggest difference between our chili and traditional versions? Instead of broth, we use tomato sauce. Or tomato soup. Or tomato paste. Or even V8.

Corn Dogs

There's almost a century of debate on the origin of this fair-food delicacy, but most agree that it's likely German in origin and a drive-in in Illinois was one of the first to shove it on a stick. Whatever the original source, Indiana fair-goers chomp them down by the millions, and they are available in virtually every mid-sized market across the state, with some of, uh, dubious quality.

Persimmon Pudding

What is persimmon pudding? Or, for that matter, what the heck is a persimmon? Imagine a tomato with the taste of an apple and the consistency of a peach. That's sort of a persimmon.

Persimmon pudding is either steamed or baked with water, much like a traditional English Christmas pudding, then served warm with whip cream. For those adhering to strict tradition, it can also be topped with a trickle of caramel brandy sauce.

Gourmet Popcorn

Sigh. What can a Hoosier say? We like our popcorn. We should, since we produce over 200 million pounds of it a year. The weirder the combination of ingredients, the better, and if you slap the word GOURMET on it, you'll really get us interested.

Deep-Fried Anything

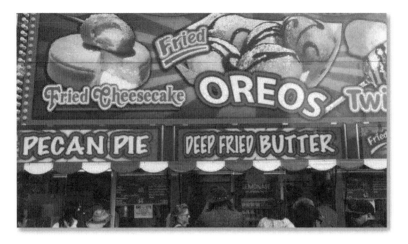

Brave Hoosiers are willing to try anything and everything dipped and fried in a variety of oils, no matter what the Surgeon General might say. We Hoosiers proudly advertise our love of deep-fried funnel cakes, elephant ears, Oreos, Twinkies, Snickers, pickles, apples, cheesecakes, White Castles, cheeseburgers, eggs...pizza...

Geez, maybe we do have a problem.

Canned Pickles

Canning is as practical and useful today as it was fifty years ago, and an art form passed down from generation to generation without gender boundaries.

In Indiana, pickles seem to be our food of choice for gourmet canning, and we've composed hundreds of variations on a seemingly combination of cucumbers, vinegar, water and salt. Garlic pickles, mustard pickles, spicy pickles, sweet & spicy pickles, super spicy pickles, peppercorn pickles...

Fried Brain Sandwiches

I...I just can't eat this. My grandmother could and my grandfather (God rest) would chow down on these until Doomsday, but I just can't eat brains and know it. That said, I suspect my grandmother might have mixed in a little pork brain with our scrambled eggs when I was a kid. She's crafty.

Anyway...some Hoosier love fried brain sandwiches. Not head cheese, mind you, but actually fried pork brain sandwiches.

Beef Manhattan

I saved the best for last.

As a kid growing up in Indiana, this was one of my favorite meals to order at a restaurant AND eat at home. A thick slice of bread, topped with a glob of mashed potatoes (skins-on preferably), then some tender roast beef and a super-generous portion of beef gravy. It was the kind of meal only a kid could enjoy, because an adult would pass out from the carbohydrate overload.

Problem is, only Indiana's older dining establishments still serve the Beef Manhattan, which I think is a cultural tragedy. When my two kids branch out in food choices, I can't wait to make it for them. Just like my dad did for me.

Indiana's Open-Air School Experiment

By Mary Giorgio

Some historians theorize that one in seven humans was killed by tuberculosis prior to the start of the twentieth century. Physicians understood little of illness and consequently believed it could be cured through rest and exposure to fresh air.

Many people with tuberculosis were confined to sanatoriums, where they were quarantined from the general population and encouraged to spend time outdoors in secluded settings. As an off chute of this movement, public health officials began to experiment with the idea that they could prevent tuberculosis from taking hold in sickly children through the same concept.

The first open-air schools debuted in Europe, but the movement soon spread to the United States. By 1908, the first open-air school had been founded in America. Indiana soon jumped on the bandwagon, opening many of these schools in the first quarter of the twentieth century.

The Indiana Society for the Prevention of Tuberculosis formed with the goal to establish the first open-air school in Indiana. They were fully endorsed by the State Board of Health. In 1913, the society partnered with the Lucretia Mott School on Indianapolis's east side to open the first open-air classroom in Indiana. They converted a regular classroom in the school for the fresh air concept.

The open-air concept was soon deployed statewide. Fort Wayne followed on the heels of Indianapolis, opening its first fresh air school. Others followed across the state, in urban and rural communities alike.

Open-air schools targeted children who were malnourished, had been exposed to tuberculosis, or were exhibiting pre-tuberculosis symptoms. Public health officials believed that exposing these children to fresh air and sunshine would prevent them from contracting tuberculosis. To aid this goal, windows were kept open year-round, even in winter.

To keep children warm in winter months, they were required to wear snowsuits in the classroom. Many of the children complained of being cold, despite the winter gear.

Unlike a regular classroom, open-air schools emphasized physical activity throughout the school day. Children participated in academics, but also spent time gardening, playing outdoors, and learning about personal hygiene. They were also served nutritious meals and provided at least one rest a day.

While academic work was included in the daily routine, it was not a focus. As a result, the schools were criticized for not being academically challenging. This would eventually be a contributing factor to their demise, in addition to their failing as a cure for tuberculosis.

Today, few people are aware of the history of the open-air school in Indiana. By the 1930s, the short reign of these schools in Indiana came to an end. Physicians had finally begun to understand the true cause of tuberculosis and thus understood that fresh air could not prevent or cure the disease. By the start of World War II, an effective antibiotic treatment for the illness had been developed.

One Hoosier, Thousands of Lives

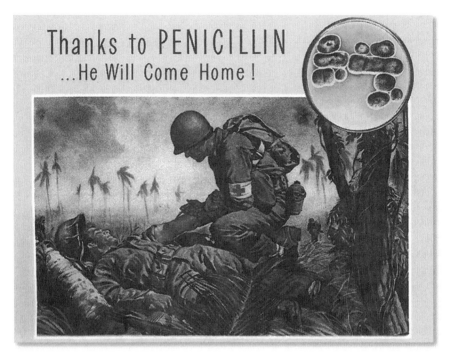

Thanks to PENICILLIN
...He Will Come Home!

By Mary Giorgio

At the dawn of World War II, the Allied troops faced a significant problem. Medical personnel needed a better method of treatment for infection, especially on the battlefield. Without the development of new drugs, thousands of men would die from their wounds.

Hoosier Andrew Jackson Moyer successfully developed the technique necessary to mass produce penicillin in time to save hundreds of thousands of lives.

Moyer was born in 1899, in Star City, Indiana. He spent his early
years living in both Star City and Logansport, before joining the
U.S. Army's Student Training Corps at Wabash College in 1918.
Moyer graduated with a bachelor's degree in 1922. He went on
to earn a master's degree from North Dakota Agricultural
College and a PhD in plant pathology from the University of
Maryland.

After graduating with his PhD, Moyer worked as a mycologist
with the U.S. Department of Agriculture. He later transferred to
the USDA Northern Regional Research Laboratory in Peoria, Ill.
It was there that Moyer would become famous for his research on
penicillin.

As rumblings of war began across Europe, scientists at Oxford
University in England were desperately searching for a reliable
treatment for battlefield infections. In the course of their
research, they stumbled upon the work of Scottish scientist

Alexander Fleming. His discovery of penicillin in 1928 showed a great deal of potential.

Lacking funds to complete further research themselves, British scientists Howard Florey and Norman Heatley embarked on a journey to bring the penicillin to America. They teamed up with the USDA to develop an effective method of large-scale penicillin production. Moyer was assigned to the team.

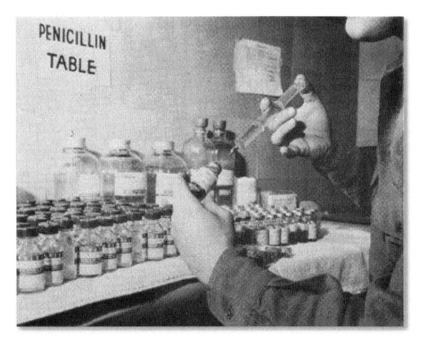

Moyer and his team made several discoveries that ultimately led to the development of a marketable penicillin product. First, Moyer discovered that corn steep liquor provided a perfect growing medium for penicillin. A byproduct of cornstarch, corn steep liquor was readily available and inexpensive to obtain.

Moyer also discovered that adding milk sugar to the growth medium further increased penicillin yields. These breakthroughs, combined with the discovery of a better strain of penicillin, resulted in the successful scale-up of drug production.

Soon, American manufacturers were producing large quantities of the drug. By D-Day in June 1944, battlefield hospitals had ample supplies of the valuable drug. The ability to mass produce penicillin for treatment of soldiers' wounds was a huge boon to the Allied forces.

Moyer retired in 1957 and died two years later in 1959. In 1987, he was inducted posthumously into the, the first government researcher to be so honored. Today, Moyer is remembered for his contributions to the development of penicillin. Manufacturers have been producing antibiotics like penicillin at affordable prices since the mid-1940's. His research has saved millions of military and civilian lives.

Kokomo, Indiana: The "City of Firsts"

By Tim Bean

A hundred years ago, no city in the Midwest experienced an influx of industry, ingenuity and American innovation as did Kokomo, Indiana. Riding off the fumes of Indiana's brief natural gas boom, inventors and industrialists alike met in the city and cranked out invention after invention. This parade of progress earned Kokomo the title "City of Firsts."

The First Push-Button Car Radio

Before the push-button radios, drivers tuned car audio the old-fashioned way—by searching the squeaks and squelches of AM signals with a knob. The Delco Division of General Motors in

Kokomo released a push-button radio in 1938, allowing drivers to "program" stations.

The World's First Pneumatic Tire

To combat the rough terrain of America's earliest roads, D.C. Spracker of the Kokomo Rubber Tire Company invented the pneumatic tire in 1894, inflating an amalgam of rubber and fabric around a rim.

First Aerial Bomb with Fins

To improve the increasing tactical use of aircraft, Kokomo's Liberty Pressed Metal Company introduced the first bomb with aerial fins in 1918, allowing greater accuracy and reliability in aerial bombardment.

The First Mechanical Corn Picker

Front View of JOHN POWELL PICKER

Known as the John Powell Picker (named after its inventor), there can hardly be an invention more suited for use in Indiana. Powell

220

had been attempting to build a better tractor, but witnessed how corn harvesters floundered in the muddy terrain of cornfields. He then created the two-row corn picker in 1920, a PTO implement for contemporary tractors.

The First "McDiner"

In an effort to expand its services and market, McDonald's briefly toyed with the idea of a "McDiner", allowing families to enjoy McDonald's food in a full-service, casual dining atmosphere. The first "McDiner" popped up in Kokomo in 2001. The idea never caught on.

The First Stainless Steel Flatware

In 1912, prolific (and amateur) Indiana scientist Elwood Haynes perfected the first flatware composed of stainless steel, satisfying his wife's request for dining utensils that didn't tarnish or taste funky. His invention eventually became part of the Haynes Stellite Company, a producer of industrial metals and also flatware.

The First Canned Tomato Juice

Although Kokomo's credit for the first canned tomato juice is sometimes questioned, the town's proximity to the French Lick Springs Hotel, where the drink first became popular as a cocktail ingredient, makes it the most likely candidate. Kokomo's Kemp Brothers Canning Company created a canned version of tomato juice in 1928 not for businessmen, but for babies.

Evansville's Legendary Bosse Field

By Zach Hoom

When asked about iconic ballparks, most baseball fans will gravitate towards Boston's Fenway Park or Chicago's Wrigley Field. For good reason. These historic stadiums are certainly worthy of their status - the Green Monster at Fenway and Wrigley's ivy-covered outfield walls have been etched into the memories of baseball fans across the country.

Ask about the *third* most iconic baseball diamond and the answer isn't quite so cut and dry. The new Yankee Stadium is a modern imitation of the old Yankee Stadium, Camden Yards looks old (but isn't), the original Comiskey Park was demolished in 1991 (and its replacement has since been renamed). With the exception of 1960's Dodger Stadium and Kansas City's Kaufman Field, the remaining "old" stadiums in the big leagues are mostly sleek eyesores from the 1990s.

The question might stump fans nationwide, but in Evansville, Indiana, the answer is pretty clear: Bosse Field, home of the Independent Frontier League's Evansville Otters.

Since opening its doors to a then-record 8,082 fans on June 17, 1915, Bosse Field has continuously housed minor league pro teams for over a century. It's the third oldest in-use professional baseball field in the United States, trailing only Fenway (1912) and Wrigley (1914).

The field was also the first municipally-owned professional sports stadium in the country, named after former mayor Benjamin Bosse, a man instrumental in the stadium's approval and development.

Over the years, the stadium has hosted a wide variety of minor league baseball teams and one (pre-merger) NFL football team. The first inhabitants of the stadium, the Evansville River Rats, won the Central League Championship in 1915, the only year they played at Bosse. Since then, teams have won 9 more championships – most recently, the Evansville Otters won in 2016.

Between 1926 and 1984, a series of major league affiliated teams and future MLB players played at Boose Field. Most notably, Hall of Famer Hank Greenberg played for the Evansville Hubs in 1931, back when he was a prospect in the Detroit system. In the 1970s and early '80s, the AAA Evansville Triplets served as the top affiliate for the Minnesota Twins (1970), Milwaukee Brewers (71-73) and the Detroit Tigers (74-84).

Ironically, with all due respect to Hank Greenberg, the most celebrated residents of Bosse weren't baseball players at all, but actors. In 1992, the field was extensively used for the filming of 'A League of their Own', starring Tom Hanks Geena Davis, and Madonna.

Made in America, Made in Indiana

By Tim Bean

In 2018, *Site Selection Magazine,* a periodical dedicated to the past, present, and future of corporate real estate, ranked Indiana #8 for Business Climate. This ranking combined averaged numerous factors, including the opinion of executives, competitiveness, and taxation. For those in and out of Indiana business, whether large or small, that's no great surprise: the Hoosier State wants to attract and keep entrepreneurs.

That hard-working spirit has threaded itself into the DNA of Indiana culture through centuries of manufacturers and industries, some of which have become iconic American products. Here's a few you might recognize.

Bar Keepers Friend

In 1882, an Indianapolis chemist concocted a powdered cleaner using oxalic acid as a primary ingredient. Originally marketed to saloons in central Indiana, it is now a popular cleaner across the United States. Indiana-based SerVaas Laboratories now produces approximately 60,000 cans a day.

Clabber Girl Baking Powder

In the late 1700s, bakeries discovered that by adding potash (a mixture of salt and potassium) to bread, you could increase its volume and soften its texture. At first, cooks made this concoction at home (a lengthy process), but some companies began manufacturing this "baking powder".

In the late 1800s, Clabber Girl Baking Powder emerged, becoming the most recognized brand of baking powder. With simple ingredients and an iconic can design (the drawing has remained unchanged since 1940), Clabber Girl is manufactured in Terre Haute by Hulman & Company.

Red Gold Tomatoes

In 1942, the Hutcherson family saw potential in a partially-burned cannery in Orestes, Indiana. After restoring the cannery and planting hundreds of acres of tomatoes around it, they started a canned tomato company known

first as "Indiana's Finest" and then "Indiana Chef."

After three decades of astounding growth, the family renamed it Red Gold Tomatoes, one of the largest canned tomato companies in the United States. Red Gold cans and processes 80% of the tomatoes grown in the Midwest today. The company now has over 2,000 employees and is headquartered in Elwood, Indiana.

The Saturday Evening Post

Few periodicals are as emblematic of Americana as *The Saturday Evening Post*. Its unique combination of informative articles, fiction, illustrations and literary hodge-podge transformed it into the most popular general interest magazine in the United States. Sadly, its throne was stolen by the rise of television, and its publishers announced the final issue in 1969.

Indianapolis entrepreneur Beurt SerVaas purchased the Post's publishing company in 1970 and relaunched it as a quarterly, retaining the same folksy nostalgia that defined the original magazine. Today, the magazine is published six times a year by the Saturday Evening Post Society, an Indianapolis-based nonprofit.

Hoosier Bat Company

26 years ago, Valparaiso resident Dave Cook, a former scout for the New York Yankees, decided to manufacture a baseball bat composed of wood but mimicking the lighter weight of an aluminum bat. His three-piece bat was named the Woodforce 2000, and it launched the Hoosier Bat Company.

Although many Hoosiers Bats make the rounds in Major League Baseball, Dave Cook discovered a much larger niche, marketing his bats to youth, high school, and college programs. Today, the Indiana company is one of the Midwest's most popular baseball bat manufacturers.

Batesville Casket Company

In 1906, John A Hillenbrand purchased the flagging Batesville Coffin Company and renamed it the Batesville Casket Company, transforming a failing business into one of America's leading suppliers of funerary products (coffins had fallen out of vogue).

Never a company to rest on simple success, Hillenbrand and Batesville expanded with innovation and diversification. Now a publicly-traded company on the New York Stock Exchange, Hillenbrand, Inc. (HI) retained its Hoosier roots, maintaining headquarters in Batesville, Indiana.

Autocar Company

Founded in 1897, the Autocar Company of Hagerstown, Indiana, remains the oldest active motor vehicle manufacturer in the Western Hemisphere. Autocar actually made its last "car" in 1911 and today specializes in industrial or commercial vehicles.

During World War II, the company provided the US Army with a variety of military vehicles, including half-tracks.

With a focus on customer needs, the Hagerstown plant manufacturers Class 8 vehicles customized for specific use, often in severe-duty settings. Several cities—Miami, Chicago and Houston among them—depend on the Autocar Company's vehicles for almost all municipal functions, from aircraft support to refuse trucks.

Action Custom Straps

What do Travis Tritt, Billy Corgan, and Jimmy Buffet have in common? For one, they all use Action Custom Straps, a legendary guitar strap manufacturer in Indianapolis. Starting in 1978, Action Custom Straps were founded by the Misner family, who sought to make a heavy-duty camera strap that could be worn comfortably.

The straps were well-received, but the company closed its doors in 1986, finding the market too small and the ordering process too ungainly. The company reopened in 1999, this time focusing on the guitar strap market and using the Internet as a tool for both ordering and advertising. Professional and amateur guitar players esteem the handmade straps today.

Zombie-Style History: Exploring Abandoned Indiana

By Tim Bean

When I say "zombie-style" I don't literally mean brain-munching zombies, folks. I refer to once-used-now-abandoned buildings. We should make that clear.

Before I start rolling these Indiana sites, let's get the obligatory disclaimer out of the way. Whether an urban explorer or history junkie, I am in *no way* recommending you actually trespass upon these properties. Hoosier hospitality is a real thing, but so is Hoosier firearm appreciation.

That said, if you can contact the owner of the property, offer a small gratuity. You'd be amazed at how friendly people become when you're polite, honest, and willing to hand them $20. I know

this firsthand. Slipping through a broken fence, at night, in secret, might be thrilling, but so is a double-load of buckshot to the ass. Just saying.

Reid Memorial Hospital in Richmond

The story of Reid Memorial Hospital is the story of hundreds of hospitals across the country: built a century earlier, modified, expanded and updated until the cost of modernization caught up. Then abandoned.

Reid Memorial lasted longer than most. Built in 1905, it held on until 2008. Potential buyers came and went and then stopped coming all together. Nature's reclamation happened quickly, and the hospital soon looked like a fifty-year derelict. Demolition began in spring of 2018, but portions of the campus still remain.

Abandoned Dome Cabin in Bloomington

I visited this nugget several years ago. As far as I know it's still standing, but considering its placement, vandalism and exposure, I'm sure it's time is limited. There's not as much history as story in this abandoned dome cabin. Once upon a time, a lot of love went into its construction.

The walls were made of heavy-duty fiberglass, which explains why it's still standing. Its expansive three-seasons room would have been perfect for lazy days in the outdoors or fly-free dining. It had a basement for storage, a shower and even skylights. This was "glamping" even before the term was invented.

If you'd like to find it, it's near the Cutright State Recreation Area in Bloomington, just off Knightridge Road. Nearby is the abandoned Zoom Floom Waterpark, so explorers could find a two-for-one deal here. Or, three-for-one, if you check out the next site.

Knightridge Space Observatory in Bloomington

Built just before World War II, the Knightridge Space Observatory was as Spartan an observatory as you could find in the US.

Housing a medium-sized refractor scope—which would be rendered virtually obsolete by the up-and-coming reflecting scopes—the observatory was a simple, circular brick building with wooden floors and dome.

In its first two or three decades, the observatory had no nearby neighbors. As housing encroached and the university expanded, so did light pollution, making it impossible for researchers to conduct serious study of deep-sky objects. Astronomers abandoned it to the elements, and it has stood in a patch of woods ever since. Weathering has made the second floor too hazardous for exploration, but the brick walls are still sound.

Salesians Preparatory School in Cedar Lake

Many Hoosier ghost hunters consider Salesians one of Indiana's great locales for discovering spectral evidence. *Sigh.* Like former asylums or hospitals, abandoned schools naturally led themselves to myth, and it's in those myths the unscrupulous harvest the gullible. There are no ghosts here, folks. Just an old school and the occasional "ghost hunter."

That said, it's an interesting place to check out. Built in the 1950s, Salesians stood as the premier Catholic school in Lake County. This didn't last and the Catholic Church closed in the school in 1979 for financial reasons.

The property's been bought and sold several times, once briefly serving as a paintball facility, but none ever lasted. Salesians Preparatory School stands off about a quarter mile off Cline Avenue in Cedar Lake.

Central State Hospital in Indianapolis

In the 1850s, this iconic hospital occupied a single building in Indianapolis, but by the 1920s it expanded to an entire campus housing over 3,000 patients.

Like many asylums in the early to mid-20th century, Central State Hospital of Indianapolis was a self-sufficient campus, complete with recreation and occupational activities for the patients, housing, ornate landscaping and food production facilities. This wasn't for the sake of progress. These facilities were designed to keep mental illness out of sight, a cultural taboo that still exists today.

After some of the oldest buildings were either repurposed or destroyed, Central State Hospital limped on until thin funding and accusations of patient abuse finally closed its doors in 1994.

Gary's Union Station

I hesitated adding this to the list; too many buildings in Gary have been targets for unscrupulous urban explorers, to the point where it's become more like picking the bones of a city than discovering history.

But Gary's Union Station is too much of a stand-out to ignore.

Union stations across the United States were modern models of architecture and attitude. The typically Art Deco or Neoclassical styles symbolized a country growing in commerce and culture, as the United States emerged from its isolationist cocoon to become a world power.

Gary's Union Station combines elements of the old and the new. Built almost immediately after JP Morgan founded the city, the concrete pillars of Union Station were first poured and then etched to mimic classic stone construction. Its placement into a hillside allowed its front portion to have two stories while having only a single story in the back.

Closed in the 1950s, it is covered head-to-toe in graffiti and not a single window remains unbroken, but its solid construction, and the help of the hillside, have kept it relatively solid, if not pretty.

Hotel Mudlavia near Kramer

At the turn of the century, the healing properties of natural springs came into vogue as a panacea for a myriad of diseases, from cancer to rheumatism. With Southern Indiana boasting several natural springs, posh resorts popped up, claiming cures with no FDA to countermand them. Some, like the West Baden Springs Hotel, still welcome thousands of visitors a year. Others, like the Hotel Mudlavia, simply faded away...

The Hotel Mudlavia opened in 1890 and cost a quarter of a million to build, which would equal almost $10 million today. For three decades, the hotel served a steady stream of the well-to-do, the chronically sick, and the occasional Indiana celebrity, such as James Whitcomb Riley.

Unfortunately a fire gutted the building in 1930. It took several years to reopen as a rest home and then a lodge. When its owners decided to revisit its former glory and renamed it "Mudlavia Lodge"...it burned down yet again.

The Sweet, Stinky, and Sticky Life of Maple Syrup

By Tim Bean

I am always amazed that people are amazed by the process of making maple syrup, traditionally known as sugaring.

Amazed by the questions I receive from visitors, amazed so many think sugaring in their home kitchen could be profitable, and amazed so many don't know the difference between real maple syrup and tinted corn syrup (sold as "pancake syrup" with names like Aunt Jemima, Log Cabin, Hungry Jack, etc...).

Before I continue, let me offer a fair warning: if you've never had real maple syrup, and would rather not add the expense to your food budget, Don't. Even. Try. It. You'll never be able to choke down the imitation "pancake syrup" stuff ever again, even at triple the cost.

Real maple syrup is expensive because its manufacture is so time-consuming, but comparing it to the tinted corn syrup is like comparing real oxygen to imitation oxygen. The difference is that dramatic. Even chemists admit they cannot replicate the taste of maple syrup accurately.

Sugaring goes a little something like this: You find a silver, red or sugar maple. You tap that maple tree (punch a small tube into it) and hook a collection receptacle to it, a bucket, a bag or tubing that leads to a large barrel. Every day, or every few days, you collect the sap. The weather needs to be below freezing at night and above freezing during the day, so always in late winter, early spring. Once the weather gets too warm, and the tree decides it's spring, it's over. At that point the sap will taste like sour clay.

Finding and tapping the trees is the easiest part of the entire process. Sap collection, not so much. Sap is mostly water, but freezing cold water that makes your gait awkward when carried to the tank behind a four-wheel drive Gator. Even with the grace of Baryshnikov, you're going to trip and get doused with sap on a regular basis.

That freezing cold sap, just above freezing, splashes down your collar, up your sleeves and soaks through your coat and shirt. It will dry, of course, and that's when you notice it's not water, because now you're sticky. Your collar will feel like the inside of a Coke can the rest of the day.

After amassing a few hundred gallons, you're ready to cook that sap in the evaporator, a behemoth boiling tray that consumes wood like a wildfire. It heats a hundred gallons of sap to 219 degrees in a process that is more juggling than agriculture.

Check sap level, add water, check temp, slow fire, check sap level, check that valve, open this valve, close that valve, shift wood, add sap, add water, check sap level…for hours and days, moving in a steady, careful circle around the evaporator, careful not to trip over the pile of wood by the oven doors, wiping the sticky steam from your forehead. The curtain of stream is so thick you need a powerful narrow-beam flashlight to cut through it and check the sap level.

If that sap gets too low…oh, that's something you never want to think about. It's a China syndrome on a small scale. The fierce heat of the wood fire becomes absorbed by the metal of the evaporator pans instead of being safely dissipated by the boiling water. The stainless steel evaporator heats, then burns, then collapses into a six-thousand dollar pile of scrap metal. Typically you have a hose attached to the evaporator to add water. If the hose doesn't work, I keep a five-gallon bucket nearby and there's a river ten yards away. Just in case.

As long as you can avoid that, you pour off the hot syrup into metal buckets, then carry those heavy buckets to a filtering station. You might slosh once, but you'll never do it again.

Scalding hot syrup sticks to your skin and is a great reminder to be careful. Filter it once, twice, then leave it in a steel container to cool. Then do it again. And again. For hours, days, weeks, as long as the sap is running from your tapped maple trees. After a few days, the world outside the sugar shack feels as distant as Jupiter.

You stop noticing the salty-smoke smell of a burning wood fire or the sweet tang of maple syrup. Visitors always notice it. In fact, they often visit the sugar shack simply for that smell. But there's one smell you never forget—bad sap. The stink of bad sap borders on Biblical.

Once collected, you have approximately one week to cook sap before it turns to the darkside. This can change depending on temperature (warmer weather equals less time). Leave a tank of sap in the hot sun for a day, and you'll ruin the entire batch in twenty-four hours.

Fresh sap has almost no smell, just a very faint woodsy odor like newly-fallen leaves. But after five days, you'll notice the tiniest tinge of fermentation, like a beer poured across the room. It's still okay, but that's the sap's way of giving you a swift kick in the butt. In only a day or two, that smell gets funkified fast. It turns into an unforgettable amalgam of cheesy, putrid sweetness (I literally just shuddered thinking about it as I wrote). The sap turns a cloudy yellow of mustard gas.

Believe me, if you ever accidentally fill up an evaporator with bad sap and then have to spend the next three hours emptying, hosing and scrubbing the metal pans to banish it, you'll remember. A stench like that tends to tattoo itself in your memory. I speak from experience.

In closing, be assured I am not complaining. Every industry, from teaching to toll booth operating, has its pluses and minuses. I enjoy making maple syrup, especially on a smaller-scale, without the quotas and pressures of big business, but it's not an idyllic endeavor. Many sugaring newbies think it is. It takes time, time and more time.

It's easier to buy a bottle from the store and read a few articles on sugaring rather than attempting it yourself. I can say this: I have never met a single person who actually processed syrup from tree to table and say it was easy. However, it's probably the best-tasting hobby in the world.

Lassen Pavilion and Indiana's Early "Party Town"

LASSEN BROS.' PAVILION.
Cedar Lake, Ind.

By Mary Giorgio

In the decades between 1890 and 1940, Lake County's Cedar Lake was a popular resort town frequented by Chicagoans looking for a weekend getaway. The town had everything folks from the Windy City wanted – a nice beach, clear waters, leisure activities, and nighttime entertainment. Plus, it was just a short train ride away. There were even rumors during Prohibition that the town was a good place to get a stiff drink. It was very true.

The town of Cedar Lake was founded in the mid-1800s. It wasn't until the Monon Railroad was extended to Cedar Lake in 1882 that tourists began to visit the area. Many locals, including

248

WE HAVEN'T HIT A DRY SPOT YET

in CEDAR LAKE, IND.

Christian Lassen, saw an opportunity to capitalize on this demand. At one time, 47 hotels operated in Cedar Lake.

Lassen was born in Chicago to immigrant parents in 1875. The family later moved to Cedar Lake, where he found work in the steamboat business. Around 1903, Lassen opened a dance pavilion that attracted quite a crowd. In 1919, he made the bold decision to expand his offerings.

LASSEN'S HOTEL

Lassen purchased a boarding house from Philip Armour, a meat packer from Chicago who had formerly operated an ice harvesting business on Cedar Lake. That winter, Lassen attached runners to the bottom of the boarding house and slid it across the large lake to its new home on the lake's east side.

Lassen spent the next year renovating the structure. Supposedly, project costs were close to $100,000. On Saturday, May 7, 1921, Lassen's Pavilion opened to great fanfare. The building included a 74-room hotel, each with its own private bath, a waterfront restaurant, and a dance pavilion. The resort also offered live music, boating, and fishing expeditions. The grand opening celebration featured a performance by the Ted Lewis Orchestra, one of Chicago's most famous jazz bands.

The Lassen Pavilion operated seasonally until after World War II. By then, Cedar Lake had fallen out of vogue as a weekend getaway spot. Lassen sold the building to the Lake Region Christian Assembly for use as a church camp. He moved to Florida in 1950 and died there in 1955.

The town of Cedar Lake later purchased the 20-acre property, including Lassen Pavilion. The building was scheduled for demolition when a group of concerned citizens formed the Cedar Lake Historical Association to save it. The group restored the old resort, turning it into a historical museum. It was listed on the National Register of Historic Places in 1981.

Today, the Lake of the Red Cedars Historical Museum tells the story of the once-famous resort town. Visitors can learn about Cedar Lake's unique history while enjoying a tour of the restored hotel and restaurant. The museum is open on weekends from May to September.

Thornless Roses and the Krider World's Fair Garden of Middlebury

By Mary Giorgio

Nestled in the community of Middlebury, Indiana, sits Krider World's Fair Garden, a park featuring display and botanic gardens originally conceived for the 1933 Chicago World's Fair. The garden was the brainchild of Vernon Krider, owner of a wholesale and mail-order nursery. Following the end of the fair, Krider transported his display to Middlebury, where it has remained for the past 85 years.

Vernon Krider began his nursery in 1894. That year, his father gifted him with two acres of land following his high school graduation. Krider planted small berry plants on the land, letting them grow, and cultivating cuttings to begin his nursery. He made his first sale in 1896: $25 for 5,000 raspberry plants. Over time, Krider purchased more land and expanded his offerings. While his business originally began as a wholesale nursery, Krider eventually expanded into mail-order sales. In fact, Krider ran one of the earliest mail-order nurseries in the United States.

The 1933 World's Fair came at the perfect time for the business. Krider saw the display garden as an opportunity to expand the national market for his mail-order nursery.

The 1933 Chicago World's Fair, also known as the "Century of Progress International Exposition," commemorated the 100th anniversary of the founding of the City of Chicago. The hottest technology of its day dominated displays, including the famed diesel-powered Zephyr and an extravagant $1.4 million passenger car. Every aspect of the fair was designed to promote feelings of optimism and wonder at what the future might hold (sadly, World War II would erupt six years later).

Although the country was in the midst of the worst economic crisis in memory, the fair was tremendously successful. Originally scheduled to last just one year, organizers decided to continue the fair through 1934 in response to great demand. It is estimated that over 48 million people visited the exhibits between 1933 and 1934.

Krider's decision to participate in the fair turned out to be a savvy business move. He spent over $10,000 on plants and decorations for his display garden. "Krider's Diversified Garden" became a popular stop for fairgoers. By the time the fair ended in 1934, he had collected a whopping 250,000 names and addresses of potential customers for his mail-order business.

Krider's nursery flourished during the next few decades. At its peak, its grounds covered 420 acres and had over 100 employees. It became the largest employer in town with orders so numerous the Middlebury Post Office had to expand to meet the demand.

In 1945, Krider patented the *Festival*, the first thornless rose in the United States. Roses thereafter became a big business for the nursery. Krider roses were so popular that in 1971, President Nixon's daughter Tricia Nixon used them for her wedding ceremony.

Beginning in the 1980s, big-box chains began to take business from local operations like Krider Nursery. The business was sold in 1986 amid slumping sales and eventually closed. In 1993, the Krider family donated the 2.4-acre World's Fair Garden to the town of Middlebury.

Today, visitors can still see the original waterwheel, windmill, and the giant toadstool that were on display at the Chicago World's Fair in 1933. The enchanting garden also features walking paths and a giant quilt garden, with flowers planted in a unique quilt pattern. It is a favorite spot among locals and tourists alike.

The Unsolved Murder of Dr. Helen Knabe

By Mary Giorgio

A trailblazing female physician, Helene Knabe was living her dream of practicing medicine when, on the morning of October 23, 1911, she was found dead. The mystery surrounding her death baffled investigators. Although they pursued several leads and even indicted one man, in the end, Dr. Knabe's murderer was never brought to justice.

Dr. Helene Knabe immigrated to America from Prussia in 1896. For several years, she worked in domestic labor to learn English and save enough money to enroll in medical school. In 1900, Knabe was accepted to the Medical College of Indiana. There, her dedication and talent were soon recognized by an appointment as curator of the school's pathology lab. She was also the only student selected by the Director of Pathology to teach courses to underclassmen.

MEDICAL COLLEGE OF INDIANA (NOW A GREAT MUSEUM IN INDY)

Dr. Knabe graduated on April 22, 1904. She was one of two female graduates that year. Dr. Knabe continued working as lab curator and clinical professor at the college. In 1905, she became the first woman in Indiana to be appointed Assistant Deputy State Health Officer. Dr. Knabe became a leading expert on rabies prevention. She was later promoted to acting superintendent but resigned when the State Board of Health refused to offer her pay equal to her male counterparts.

After resigning, Dr. Knabe opened a private practice and became the medical director and associate professor of physiology and hygiene at the Normal College of the National American Gymnastics Union. Through her association with Dr. William B.

Craig, Dean of Students at the Indiana Veterinary College, Dr. Knabe was appointed Chair of Hematology and Parasitology at the school in 1909.

DELAWARE FLATS WHERE DR. KNABE LIVED

There were rumors of a romance between Craig and Knabe, with some suggestion that an engagement may have been called off shortly before her murder. She had confided her engagement to a friend and sales records showed that she had recently commissioned a possible wedding gown.

On the morning of October 23, 1911, Dr. Knabe's laboratory assistant entered her rooms at the Delaware Flats apartment complex and found Dr. Knabe lying on the bed with her throat slit. By the time police arrived an hour later, the crime scene had been disturbed by numerous gawkers. This, coupled with accusations that police officers failed to take the investigation seriously, hampered detectives' ability to solve the crime. Indianapolis Police Chief Martin Hyland publicly suggested she had committed suicide, based on the assumption that Dr. Knabe was large enough to ward off an attacker. Coroner Charles Durham quickly laid this claim to rest, noting defensive wounds on the victim and the absence of a plausible suicide weapon.

DOCTOR IS SLAIN

Helen Knabe of Indianapolis Is Murdered in Her Bed.

WEAPON USED IS MISSING

Former State Bacteriologist Is Found With Her Head Nearly Severed From Body—No Motive for Crime Can Be Traced.

Newspapers were quick to sensationalize the murder, and Dr. Knabe was subjected to attacks on her character. As a single, 35-year-old female physician who demanded equality, Dr. Knabe defied society's gender norms as a proud suffragette. The public found it easier to blame the gruesome murder on her "unwomanly" lifestyle.

Dr. Knabe was buried in an unmarked grave in Crown Hill Cemetery. Fifteen months later, two men were indicted: Dr. William B. Craig for murder and Alonzo M. Ragsdale, Dr. Knabe's business partner and executor, as an accessory-to-murder. At trial, the state's case quickly fell apart for lack of evidence. Dr. Craig was acquitted and charges against Ragsdale were dropped.

Dr. Knabe's murder remains unsolved. Westfield author Nici Kobrowski has researched the crime extensively, drawing the conclusion that Dr. Craig was the likely killer. In 2016, she published a book entitled *She Sleeps Well: the Extraordinary Life and Murder of Dr. Helene Elise Hermine Knabe*. Drawn to the doctor's unique story, Kobrowski purchased a headstone for her grave.

We will likely never know who killed Dr. Knabe. Her case file was destroyed in a flood at the Indianapolis Marion County Police Department 1977, and there is little chance that her case will ever be reopened.

AT CROWN HILL CEMETERY

Indiana-made Gatorade: The Go-To Drink of NFL & Elvis

By Zach Hoom

Since it first came to market in the 1960s, Gatorade has remained the #1 selling sports drink in America. Invented at the University of Florida and named for its winning Gators football team, few people know that Indiana company Stokely Van Camp played a tremendous role in the product's early development.

It all started at the University of Florida in the mid-1960s. The Gators football team faced a big problem: the summer of 1965 had been perilously hot and humid, with over 24 freshman players hospitalized for dehydration. The team had to practice daily and could not afford losing players.

A team of university researchers, led by Dr. Robert Cade, began a quest to create a sports drink for the team. The resulting product, Gatorade, reportedly hydrated players faster than water. More focused on the marketability of the product than its scientific validity, the inventors called it "Gatorade" (instead the more scientific-sounding "Gator-Aid").

Researchers knew that their product had a remarkable potential on the market. However, they had little time or knowledge of the commercialization process.

In 1967, one of the project members moved to Indiana to take a job at Indiana University. There, he met Alfred Stokely. Already in search of a fresh product to market, Stokely immediately recognized the drink's market potential (his company's signature product, Van Camp's Beans, had been on the market since the 1930s).

Stokely immediately purchased the rights to Gatorade. The drink was sold in cans, but the company switched to glass bottles due to corrosion from the beverage's high salt content. A powdered formula was later offered for convenience. Gatorade was marketed primarily to athletic teams. Almost immediately, Stokely was able to sign on as the National Football League's official sports drink.

Gatorade wasn't the first sports beverage of its kind to be developed, but its iconic success resulted from successful marketing and ordinary luck. The Gators were a winning team, and the drink's commercial launch coincided with a winning season. The team went on to win the 1969 Orange Bowl, bringing further fame to the product.

Known for its unique branding, sports teams across the country could be seen hauling orange and white coolers and green paper cups with the Gatorade logo onto the field. The drink even gained a fan club among celebrities. Elvis Presley was known to gulp Gatorade during concerts.

Seeking to capitalize on Gatorade's success, other companies attempted to bring similar products to market, but nothing could outpace Gatorade's lead in the industry. Coca-Cola finally achieved success with its Poweraid drink, but has never unseated Gatorade as the #1 seller.

In 1983, Quaker Oats purchased Stokely Van Camp for a whopping $220 million. The deal primarily sought to obtain the coveted Gatorade brand. Under the Quaker Oats umbrella, Gatorade grew substantially. In 1991, they signed Michael Jordan as the spokesperson for the iconic drink.

Today, Gatorade is owned by PepsiCo and continues to be the top seller in the sports drink industry (lemon-lime is still Gatorade's top flavor). Although the brand has changed hands several times, Gatorade remains a Hoosier product. The drink is still produced in Indianapolis at the Ameriplex Business Park.

Indiana Insects to Avoid: the Pesky, Painful, and Possibly Fatal

By Tim Bean

Before we roll out a list of the Hoosier state's most dangerous insects, let's remember that, like the vast majority of animals, insects are far more terrified of people than even our worst phobias can concoct.

To insects, we are are a clumsy, fleshy mountain of heat and noise. Our foot can destroy their entire home. Insects will do their best to run and hide from terrifying humans, with biting or stinging a desperate last resort. Except for mosquitos. Mosquitos are just awful.

If you're stepping into the Indiana outdoors this year, here's what to watch out for.

Blister beetles

A much greater hazard to horses, which may accidentally ingest the insect, the blister beetle's secretions can cause contact dermatitis in humans. Like most poisonous insects, its striking colors act as a warning to would-be predators, although the black blister beetle is common in Indiana as well.

Several countries outside the US use the chemical the blister beetle secretes, cantharidin, to remove warts; it's also known by a more familiar name in holistic circles: "Spanish fly". Blister beetles thrive in tall grass, alfalfa, weeds and among flowering plants; bees are among its favorite prey.

Brown recluse spider

Probably the most feared insect in Indiana, the brown recluse spider's size makes it easy to overlook—it rarely grows more than 3/4". Nonetheless, it sometimes injects a powerful necrotic venom when it bites.

As with most potential dangerous insects, our fears greatly outweigh the realities. Brown recluse bites are very rare, especially in Indiana. Those bitten typically report only a slight pain and mild swelling, not deep tissue necrosis.

Although they prefer the soft wood of rotting logs, they can sometimes be found in homes in dry, quiet areas: unused closets, dry basements, woodpiles and cardboard boxes.

Black widow spider

The potential danger of a North American black widow spider's bite has made it the most recognizable spider in the United States. Its black body and the signature red hourglass shape on its belly signify the species, although this only describes the females.

Three-quarters of black widow bites have no lasting effect at all, with only brief and mild pain, even if the spider injects its powerful venom. But the neurotoxin it secretes can be dangerous to large animals, especially cats and dogs and, occasionally, people.

Black widows build nests at ground level, often around dark openings or holes, with the spider waiting for prey near the web's center.

Yellow Jackets

Listing each variety of wasp and hornet in Indiana would take several articles, so we'll focus on the two most commonly confused...the yellow jacket and the honey bee. Unless protecting its queen or hive (which, in the mind of the honey bee, are the same thing), the essential honey bee will not sting. A sting means death for the honey bee, since its barbed stinger causes the pollinator to eviscerate itself.

A honey bee has a shorter, rounder body covered in dense fur. Rather than yellow, it is best described as having a light brown body, a large abdomen and short wings.

Yellow jackets, on the other hand, have bright yellow, white, and black bodies with streamlined abdomens and long wings. Rotting fruit is a favorite food of these aggressive insects. A single yellow jacket sting is painful; several stings can be dangerous, even for a human.

Red velvet ant

The red velvet ant is actually not an ant at all, but a wingless wasp. Its sting is so painful it has earned the nickname "the cow killer" for "reported" cases in which a sting has actually killed an adult bovine.

This ground-nesting insect has been studied extensively for its variety of evolutionary defenses: quick speed, hard exoskeleton, venomous bite and chemical defenses. They can be found across Indiana, but are elusive, and are easily identified by its large size (3/4") and bright coloration.

Stay well away.

Assassin bugs

Assassin bugs are typically harmless, but when threatened, it's a double-threat. Not only does it wield a massive, needle-like proboscis, but can also deliver a dose of necrotic venom and digestive juices. Usually used to paralyze and liquify the insides of another insect, this venom can be painful for humans or even dangerous, causing tissue necrosis.

A variety of the assassin bug is known as the kissing bug. It feeds on the blood of animals, and will typically seek the soft tissue in

267

or around a (sleeping) human mouth to feed. South of the Equator, these bugs have been known to pass along Chagas disease, an infection that kills almost 10,000 people a year.

Oh, and it also likes to wear the bodies of its victims.

Deer ticks

Every year, doctors and hospital report tens of thousands of cases of Lyme disease, and the deer tick remains its primary cause. They reside in wooded areas, although at only a quarter-inch when fully-grown, deer ticks are difficult to spot.

Although they are most active in the summer, they emerge in the early spring to feed and will continue feeding until autumn brings sustained cold temperatures. A single dusting of snow won't kill them off.

Preventing deer tick bites is no joke, and neither is Lyme disease. Although there's a spectrum of reactions to contracting the disease, in some humans it can cause joint pain and chronic exhaustion for up to six months. Old advice is sound advice: cover your exposed skin when trekking through densely wooded areas and wear DEET-containing bug spray.

And...mosquitos

The little old annoying mosquito is also the deadliest ANIMAL in human history. The effect of its inconvenient bite go far beyond simple scratching. It transmits hundreds of both bacterial and viral diseases, including malaria, West Nile virus, yellow fever and dengue fever, all dangerous and potentially fatal.

Most elusive is the insect's ability to thrive in almost any warm, humid environment and reproduce in abundance. Scientists have long studied a variety of methods in controlling large-scale mosquito populations, but still debate the most effective method. Some scientists have even suggested extinguishing the entire species.

As with deer ticks, the standard advice is best: protective clothing and DEET-containing spray. Also be sure to dump any standing water source, which mosquito use for reproduction.

Made in the USA
Monee, IL
08 November 2019